AF605771

A FRIDGE FULL OF IDEAS TO COOK

SAVE
FUL
A FRIDGE FULL OF
IDEAS TO COOK

Contents

9:41
SAVE FUL
SMALL BITES · BIG SAVINGS ·
Create an account
Sign in

The Saveful Kitchen

Saveful was created to help families cook smarter, save more, and make the most of what they already have in a simple, inspiring, and flexible way.

It's about saving food, saving money, and unlocking everyday creativity in the kitchen. Across Australia and around the world, families are looking for practical ways to stretch their budgets, honour the food they've already bought, and make mealtimes easier. And with the average household losing the value of one in every five shopping bags each year — often from food that's still perfectly good — we saw a powerful opportunity to help.

So Saveful began with a simple question: How can we help families save food, save money, and save time... every single day?

We know most of us don't set out to let food slip through the cracks. Life is full, things get busy, and suddenly there are forgotten veggies, half-used jars, or leftovers waiting to be brought back to life. Sometimes all you need is a little inspiration — and that's exactly where Saveful steps in.

Saveful is a simple, intuitive app that helps you turn what's already in your fridge, freezer, or pantry into something delicious. No extra shopping, no stress, and definitely no guilt. Just flexible ideas, clever swaps, and flavour-packed recipes designed to fit your real life.

Every time you cook the Saveful way, you're saving money, saving food, and saving time — while also honouring the farmers who grow our food and contributing to a healthier planet. Small actions add up, and every meal becomes a chance to make a positive impact.

This book celebrates that mission. It's filled with flexible, adaptable recipes that spark creativity and make cooking feel easy and joyful. There are no strict rules, no fancy ingredients — just delicious ideas designed to work with whatever you've got.

So open the fridge, grab what's on hand, and let's turn "nothing to eat" into "something delicious"... together.

Matt Moran X Saveful

Matt has spent a lifetime championing Australian produce and the people who grow it. From his early days on the family farm to his celebrated restaurants, Matt's food philosophy has always been rooted in respect — for the ingredients, the farmers, and the stories behind every meal.

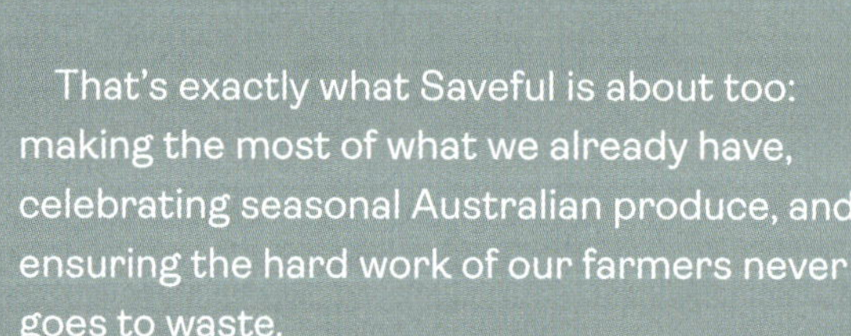

That's exactly what Saveful is about too: making the most of what we already have, celebrating seasonal Australian produce, and ensuring the hard work of our farmers never goes to waste.

Matt shares our belief that good food doesn't need to be complicated — it just needs care, creativity, and a little inspiration. Through his partnership with Saveful, Matt helps show how simple swaps, clever cooking, and a fridge-first mindset can create meals that are both delicious and mindful.

Together, we're inspiring Aussie families to cook with purpose — saving money, saving food, and saving time — while honouring the farmers, flavour, and future of Australian food.

The Saveful way

The Saveful way of cooking is a little different from your usual routine. That's because we believe great meals don't start with a shopping list — they start with the ingredients you already have. It's a more intuitive, flexible way to cook, one that's all about making the most of what's in your fridge, freezer, and pantry.

It all starts with building blocks. Throughout these pages you'll see we group ingredients, then list a host of options you can choose from, for example:

Aromatics (onion, shallot, spring onion, leek)
Fat (oil, butter, ghee)
Spices (ground cumin, ground coriander, paprika)
Sweetener (sugar, honey, maple syrup)
Flavour boosters (fresh chilli, garlic powder)

These flavour building blocks are the tools to help you create delicious, well-balanced meals with whatever ingredients you have. Sweet or savoury, simply swap out ingredients based on what's in your kitchen, your dietary needs or flavour preferences.

No stress. Just tasty food made your way to help you save money and food.

Download the Saveful app and scan the QR code on each recipe for even more flexibility.

SAVEFUL.COM

Easy and fun recipes to get the kids involved in the Saveful way of cooking.

Classic dishes that parents and kids all agree taste delicious.

Perfect for packing into lunch containers for school or work (office or home).

These recipes are suitable to store in the freezer, ready for a future meal.

Popular recipes on the Saveful app you keep coming back to time and again.

Delicious, homemade versions of your go-to takeaway favourites.

When time is not on your side, these recipes are ready to serve in 25 minutes.

Recipes you can easily prep ahead or make completely and store until serving.

Breakfast

prep + cook time 25 minutes **serves** 4

Savoury pillowy pancakes

Not into sweet? These savoury pancakes are soft, fluffy and endlessly adaptable — the perfect way to sneak in extra veg and use up whatever's in the fridge.

Ingredients

1 cup self-raising flour (see Saveful tips)

½ cup grated veggies (choose 1–3: carrot, cauliflower, zucchini), optional

⅓ cup grated or crumbled cheese (cheddar, parmesan or feta)

1–2 tbsp chopped fresh herbs (chives, dill, oregano, parsley, rosemary, thyme)

1–2 tbsp ground spices (paprika, chilli, garlic powder, onion powder), optional

¾ cup dairy or plant-based liquid (milk, cream, buttermilk, natural yoghurt or sour cream) (see Saveful tips)

1 egg or ¼ cup egg substitute

2–3 tbsp melted butter or neutral oil

finishing touches, to serve: crispy bacon, fried eggs, roasted vine ripened cherry tomatoes, and baby spinach leaves, optional

Make it

1 Preheat the oven to 150°C fan-forced. Line a baking tray with baking paper.

2 In a large bowl, add your flour. If you are using grated veggies, squeeze excess liquid from the veggies, then add to the flour along with your cheese, herbs and spices, if using. Toss them all together.

3 In a jug, whisk together your milk, egg and melted butter or oil. Gently pour your wet ingredients into your dry and stir until they are just combined. Batter should be thick but pourable; if it's too runny, add a little more flour. Don't worry about a few lumps, they make the pancakes fluffier!

4 Heat a little butter or oil in a frying pan over medium heat. Scoop about ⅓ cup of batter into pan, cooking about three at a time. Cook until bubbles appear and the edges of your pancakes look set, then flip them carefully. Cook until golden on both sides. Transfer to lined tray and keep warm in the oven. Repeat cooking pancakes in batches with remaining batter.

5 Serve your savoury pancakes stacked, topped with bacon, a fried egg, roasted tomatoes and spinach leaves, if using.

STORE Keep pancakes in an airtight container in the freezer for up to 3 months.

If you don't have self-raising flour use plain flour mixed with 2 tsp of baking powder. Use half wholemeal flour and half white flour, if you prefer.

If you only have yoghurt or sour cream, thin it down with a little water to the consistency of thickened cream.

SABRE
P

prep time 10 minutes **serves** 4

Anytime fruit smoothie

Any fruit, any juice, any time — this smoothie is all about using what you've got and sipping it nice and cold.

Ingredients

4 cups canned fruit (peaches, apricots, pears, pineapple, fruit salad)

¾ cup frozen berries or mango

2½ cups dairy or plant-based creamy goodness (milk, natural yoghurt, custard or ice-cream)

¼ cup healthy extras (oats, nuts, protein powder or a handful of cacao nibs), optional

finishing touches, to garnish: canned fruit slices and mint leaves, optional

Make it

1 Drain your canned fruit, reserving the liquid. Pop fruit in a blender with the frozen fruit and 1 cup of reserved juice. Add your creamy goodness and any healthy extras, if using.

2 Blend it all up until it is smooth, you may need a little extra liquid if your smoothie becomes too thick.

3 Pour over ice, then finish with a slice of fruit and mint leaves, if using.

prep + cook time 35 minutes **serves** 4

Spicy granola

Small swaps, big savings. Homemade granola turns pantry bits into a crunchy, golden breakfast worth waking up for.

Ingredients

¼ cup nut or seed butter (peanut, almond, cashew, sunflower seed, or coconut oil)

½ cup sweetener (honey, maple syrup, golden syrup, or molasses)

3–4 tsp mixed ground spices (choose 2–4: cinnamon, ginger, cardamom, cloves, or nutmeg, mixed spice)

2 cups rolled oats (see Saveful tips)

¼ cup seeds (pepitas, sunflower seeds, flax seeds, chia seeds, sesame seeds, or hemp seeds), optional

1 cup nuts (almonds, pecans, walnuts, cashews, or macadamias), optional

1 cup dried fruit & coconut (sultanas, raisins, currants, dried apricots, cranberries, figs, mango, pineapple, goji berries, coconut flakes), optional

Make it

1 Preheat the oven to 160°C fan-forced. Line a large baking tray with baking paper.

2 In a large bowl, combine your nut or seed butter with your sweetener and stir through until everything is well combined. Stir in your spices, taste and adjust to your liking.

3 Fold through the oats. Mix in your seeds, nuts, dried fruit or coconut, if using. Spread your mixture evenly on the tray.

4 Bake for 20–25 minutes, until it is golden and smelling warm and spicy. Make sure you keep a close eye on it so it doesn't burn, stirring once or twice. Once your granola is cooked, let it cool completely — it will crisp up as it cools.

5 Serve it your way: with milk, yoghurt, sprinkled over porridge, or simply by the handful for a delicious snack.

STORE Keep granola in an airtight jar for up to 1 month or freeze for up to 3 months.

Saveful tips

For a gluten free version swap rolled oats for quinoa flakes, brown rice flakes, or brown rice puffs.

Seasonal swaps: For winter vibes use dried figs, apples, pears, or cranberries. For summer feels, use dried mango, pineapple, apricots, sultanas.

prep + cook time 25 minutes **serves** 2

Level up scrambled eggs

Take your eggs from basic to brilliant — load them up with cheese, herbs, or fridge finds for a breakfast, lunch or dinner that saves more than just hunger.

Ingredients

4 eggs

½ cup dairy or plant-based liquid (cream, milk, buttermilk, sour cream or crème fraîche) (see Saveful tips)

3–4 tbsp neutral oil or butter

½ cup diced cured meat (bacon, ham, chorizo, pancetta, salami, or sausage), optional

1–2 tbsp finely chopped aromatics (onion, shallot, green onion, leek)

1 cup finely sliced veggies (choose 1–3: kale, spinach, zucchini, peas, broccoli, asparagus)

1–2 tsp flavour booster, to taste (chilli flakes, smoked paprika, ground cumin), optional

½ cup crumbled cheese (feta, goat cheese or ricotta)

finishing touches, to serve: fresh parsley or dill leaves, and lemon wedges

Make it

1 Let's get cracking on with your egg mixture! In a large bowl, whisk your eggs with your cream or milk and season with salt and pepper.

2 Heat 2–3 tbsp of the oil or butter in a large frying pan. Add cured meats, if using, and fry until browned. Using a slotted spoon, transfer them to a plate and set aside.

3 Add your aromatics to the pan and cook gently for 4–5 minutes until soft and fragrant. Add veggies and your flavour booster, if using, then cook until they are just tender about 3–4 minutes. Transfer your mixture to a bowl.

4 It's time to scramble. Wipe out your pan and add the remaining 1 tbsp oil or butter, then pour in the egg mixture. Let it sit for 30 seconds, then gently push from the edges to the centre, folding until just set, about 3–4 minutes.

5 Fold through your cooked veggies and cooked meat, if using. Scatter with crumbled cheese. Serve your scrambled eggs finished with a scattering of fresh herbs and lemon wedges.

Saveful Tips

If you're using sour cream or crème fraîche, thin it down with a little water to the consistency of thickened cream.

Adding cured meats to your scramble will add flavour and texture to your eggs.

Cook your eggs slightly less than you prefer as they will keep cooking all the way to the table, so by the time you eat them, they'll be perfect!

¼ CUP · 60ml
⅓ CUP · 80ml

prep + cook time 1 hour 20 minutes **makes** 1 loaf

Banana bread

Banana bread is the classic flex bake — you can swap flours, mix in nuts, choc chips, or even a swirl of Nutella. One bowl with endless possibilities.

Ingredients

3 over-ripe bananas

1 egg or ¼ cup egg substitute

½ cup neutral oil or melted butter

⅓ cup dairy or plant-based liquid (milk, cream, buttermilk, natural yoghurt or sour cream)

1 tsp ground spice (choose 1–2: cardamom, cinnamon, nutmeg, or mixed spice), optional

1½ cups self-raising flour (white, wholemeal or gluten free) (see Saveful tips)

¾ cup sugar (caster or brown)

¾ cup mix-ins (choose 2–3: chopped dried fruits, Nutella, oats, nut butter, berries, nuts, or choc chips)

1 banana, extra, peeled and halved lengthwise

Make it

1 Preheat the oven to 180°C fan-forced. Grease and line a 13.5cm x 26.5cm standard loaf tin.

2 In a large bowl, mash your bananas; you want about 1 cup of mashed banana, but a little bit more or less is ok.

3 Add your egg to the mashed banana and stir it through. Add the oil or butter and your liquid and give it a good stir until it is all mixed in. Stir in your spices, if using.

4 In a separate bowl, mix your flour and sugar. Gently fold your dry ingredients into your wet ingredients — little pockets of unmixed dry ingredients are okay, they'll help make a lighter loaf. Gently stir through most of your mix-ins, if using, leaving some for the top.

5 Spoon mixture into the prepared tin; top with halved banana, cut-side up, and scatter with any remaining mix-ins.

6 Bake for about 1 hour or until golden and a skewer comes out nice and clean. Rest loaf in the tin for about 20 minutes, then transfer to a wire rack. Serve warm or cooled.

RASPBERRY & CHOCOLATE VARIATION Replace ⅓ cup flour with ⅓ cup cocoa powder; add ½ cup fresh or frozen raspberries and ⅓ cup choc chips to the batter.

STORE Freeze slices of banana bread wrapped in plastic for up to 3 months.

Saveful Tips

This loaf can also be made into muffins. Spoon mixture into a 12-hole ⅓ cup (80ml) muffin pan and bake for 20 minutes.

Replace ⅓ cup of the flour with nut meal, cocoa, or bran, if you like.

Sautéed greens & goat cheese

prep + cook time 10 minutes **serves** 4

Toast 8 thick slices sourdough bread until golden; rub with 1–2 cloves cut garlic and drizzle with olive oil. Heat 1–2 tbsp olive oil in a frying pan on medium-high heat. Sauté 1 crushed garlic clove and 2 cups shredded kale or silverbeet for 2–3 mins, stirring occasionally until wilted. Add 2–3 tsp lemon juice to taste and season. Spread each slice of garlic toast with 1 tbsp goat cheese. Top with sautéed greens and serve with a wedge of lemon.

Tuna, white bean & chilli

prep + cook time 10 minutes **serves** 4

Toast 8 thick slices sourdough bread until golden; rub with 1–2 cloves cut garlic and drizzle with olive oil. Combine 400g can drained and rinsed cannellini beans with 1 cup rocket leaves, 2 tbsp chopped dill pickle and 1 punnet halved cherry tomatoes. Drizzle with olive oil and season; stir gently to combine. Spoon onto garlic toasts and top with drained flaked tuna. Finish with a little finely grated lemon rind.

Smashed avo with eggs

prep + cook time 10 minutes **serves** 4

Toast 8 thick slices sourdough bread until golden; rub with 1–2 cloves cut garlic and drizzle with olive oil. Coarsely mash the flesh of 2 large avocadoes in a bowl, add ½–1 tbsp lemon or lime juice and 1–2 tsp finely grated lemon or lime rind and a drizzle of olive oil. Season and mix well. Spoon avocado onto garlic toasts, top each with a halved boiled egg and scatter with chilli flakes.

Tomato & basil pesto

prep + cook time 20 minutes **serves** 4

Place 20 truss cherry tomatoes in a baking dish, combine with 1 tbsp oil; roast at 200°C fan-forced for 10 minutes until blistered. Toast 8 thick slices sourdough bread until golden; rub with 1–2 cloves cut garlic and drizzle with olive oil. Place tomatoes on garlic toast with 1–2 torn bocconcini and 2–3 tsp basil pesto. Drizzle with extra virgin olive oil and season with cracked black pepper.

Pea & ricotta

prep + cook time 15 minutes **serves** 4

Toast 8 thick slices sourdough bread until golden; rub with 1–2 cloves cut garlic and drizzle with olive oil. Place 1½ cups frozen peas in a heatproof bowl, cover with boiling water and stand for 2 minutes. Drain. Place peas, 1 tsp finely grated lemon rind, 1–2 tsp lemon juice and 2 tbsp ricotta in a bowl, season and crush lightly with a fork. Spread 1 cup ricotta evenly over garlic toast. Top with pea mixture; drizzle with extra virgin olive oil.

Cucumber & mint

prep + cook time 20 minutes **serves** 4

Toast 8 thick slices sourdough bread until golden; rub with 1–2 cloves cut garlic and drizzle with olive oil. Thinly slice 3 large Lebanese cucumbers and place in a bowl with 2 tbsp sliced fresh mint. Add 1 tbsp lemon juice, a pinch of sugar and a pinch of salt. Drizzle with 1 tbsp extra virgin olive oil; toss to combine. Marinate for at least 10 minutes. Pile onto garlic toasts, sprinkle with cracked black pepper and scatter with more mint.

prep + cook time 2 hours **serves** 8–10

Savoury avocado loaf

Do all your avos ripen at once? Don't panic — use them to make this delish super-savvy avo loaf. Over-ripe works a treat.

Ingredients

1 cup avocado flesh (about 2 small avocadoes), mashed or leftover guacamole (see Saveful tips)

3 eggs or egg substitute

¾ cup dairy or plant-based liquid (milk, cream, natural yoghurt or sour cream)

1 tsp flavour booster (finely grated lemon, lime or orange rind), optional

2 cups self-raising flour (white, wholemeal or gluten free)

2–3 tsp coarsely crushed spices (choose 1–2: caraway seeds, cumin seeds, chilli flakes, dukkah, coriander seeds, or za'atar)

1 cup grated or crumbled cheese (cheddar, parmesan, feta)

1 cup coarsely grated veggies (broccoli, carrot, cauliflower, zucchini, pumpkin or corn kernels), (see Saveful tips), optional

2–3 tbsp mixed seeds (pepitas, sunflower and sesame seeds)

finishing touches, to serve: mashed avocado, poached eggs, crumbled feta, bacon, baby spinach leaves and lemon wedges, optional

Make it

1 Preheat oven to 180°C fan-forced. Grease and line a 13.5cm x 26.5cm standard loaf tin with baking paper.

2 In a small bowl, whisk your avocado, eggs, milk, and flavour booster, if using, until combined.

3 In a large bowl, combine your flour and spices. Add your wet mixture to your dry ingredients and stir gently until everything is just combined; lumpy bits are okay. Fold in three-quarters of your cheese and the grated veggies, if using.

4 Spoon mixture into your prepared tin, smooth the top, and sprinkle over seeds and your remaining cheese. Bake for about 40–45 minutes, or until golden, risen, and the centre springs back when pressed. Cool in the tin for 10 minutes, then transfer your loaf to a wire rack.

5 Cut loaf into slices and enjoy warm or at room temperature, served with mashed avocado, poached eggs, crumbled feta, bacon, spinach leaves and lemon wedges, if using.

STORE Freeze loaf slices individually wrapped in plastic wrap for up to 3 months.

Saveful Tips

If you don't have quite enough avo, top it up with mayonnaise, aïoli, or a splash of olive oil.

Squeeze grated carrot or zucchini in paper towel to remove excess moisture. This will prevent things from going soggy.

Add extra flavour by adding up to ½ cup chopped herbs, bacon or chorizo to the batter.

prep time 15 minutes + overnight soaking **serves** 4

Overnight oats

Overnight oats are the hero of breakfast prep — cool, creamy and endlessly flexible. Prep a batch ahead, swap in any milk, yoghurt, or fruit you've got, and wake up to a feel-good start to the day (no cooking!).

Ingredients

1 cup rolled oats

1–1½ cups dairy or plant-based milk, yoghurt (see Saveful tips)

1–2 tbsp sweetener (maple syrup, honey, golden syrup), to taste

½–1 cup chopped fruit (apple, bananas, pears and fresh or frozen berries), optional

2–3 tsp flavouring (choose 2–3: cocoa, ground cinnamon, vanilla, ground nutmeg), to taste

½–1 cup crunch (almonds, pecans, walnuts, cashews, or macadamia, pepitas or sunflower seeds)

finishing touches, to serve: yoghurt, fresh strawberries, raspberries, sliced banana, macadamias, granola, and honey, optional

Make it

1 Place your oats in a large container. Pour in your milk, add the sweetener and stir to combine. The mixture should look quite wet, it will thicken as it soaks. Stir through your fruit, if using. Add your flavouring and crunch ingredients.

2 Most of your work is done and it's time to chill. Cover and pop in the fridge overnight (or for at least 6 hours) to let the oats soak and soften.

3 In the morning, check the consistency of your oats — if you like it looser, stir in an extra splash of milk. Spoon oat mixture into bowls and finish with yoghurt, strawberries, raspberries, sliced banana, macadamias, granola, and honey, if using.

STORE Keep overnight oats in a sealed container in the fridge for 3–4 days.

Saveful Tips

Use a combination of milk and yoghurt for a creamier finish or substitute milk with apple juice for a sweeter, lighter result.

DIFFERENT FLAVOUR COMBINATIONS

Lamington Add cocoa, coconut, cacao nibs, maple syrup and raspberries to the mix; serve topped with extra raspberries, cacao nibs and coconut.

Tropical Add mashed banana, chia seeds, vanilla and coconut to the mix; serve topped with mango, papaya and coconut, with a squeeze of lime.

prep + cook time 1 hour **serves** 6

Breakfast tart

This tart is perfect for clearing the fridge — tomatoes, bacon, eggs, cheese, even leftover veg all come together in a golden, flaky pastry.

Ingredients

- 1 large (30cm x 40cm) piece or 2 square sheets frozen shortcrust or puff pastry, just thawed
- 1 tbsp neutral oil
- 2 tbsp finely chopped aromatics (onion, shallots, spring onion, leek)
- 1–2 cloves garlic, finely grated or 1 tsp garlic paste
- 1 cup fresh veggies (chopped capsicum and halved cherry tomatoes)
- 2–3 rashers streaky bacon or 100g thick sliced ham, cut into thick strips
- ¼ cup leafy greens (baby spinach leaves, sliced kale, rocket, sliced silverbeet), optional
- 6 eggs
- 200g sour cream, crème fraîche or softened cream cheese (see Saveful tips)
- 2 tbsp pouring or thickened cream
- 2 tsp mustard (Dijon, seeded or American mustard or mustard powder)
- ¼ cup grated or crumbled cheese (cheddar, parmesan, feta)
- finishing touches, to serve: fresh herbs (thyme, oregano, chives), optional

Make it

1 Preheat the oven to 180°C fan-forced. Grease a large 20cm x 30cm tart tin or slice pan.

2 Line your tin with the pastry, pressing it into the edges and leave the excess to hang over the sides. If using 2 square sheets, slightly overlap them first, trim to 30cm x 40cm (reserve trimmings for another use), then press into tin. Place pastry base in the fridge until you are ready to fill your tart.

3 Heat the oil in a frying pan on medium heat; cook your aromatics and garlic until fragrant. Transfer to a plate. Cook capsicum in same pan, about 2–3 minutes until slightly softened. Cool slightly.

4 Spread aromatics, cooked vegetables, tomatoes and bacon evenly over the pastry. Scatter your leafy greens over the veggies, if using.

5 Make 6 nests in the filling. Crack one egg carefully into a small bowl, keeping yolk intact. Pour the egg into one of the nests. Repeat with remaining eggs.

6 Whisk sour cream, crème fraîche or cream cheese with cream and mustard in a bowl. Pour or spoon mixture evenly over the filling, then scatter with cheese. Fold any excess pastry back in at the edges.

7 Bake your tart for 30–35 minutes or until the pastry is golden brown and the eggs are set. Serve warm or at room temperature, finished with fresh herbs, if using.

STORE Freeze tart in an airtight container for up to 3 months.

Saveful Tips

If using cream cheese, mix with a little milk to loosen to the consistency of sour cream.

Seasonal variations: Winter **sweet potato, potato & onion;** Spring **asparagus, zucchini, leek & peas;** Autumn **mushroom, capsicum & silverbeet;** Summer **tomato, basil & rocket.**

prep + cook time 20 minutes **serves** 4

Everything fritters

Got a little bit of everything left in the fridge? Toss it in. These fritters turn odds and ends into golden, crunchy bites of goodness, perfect for breakfast or a little bite to accompany a cold drink.

Ingredients

3 cups veggies (fresh or frozen corn kernels, grated zucchini, thinly sliced kale or silverbeet)

½ cup mixed finely sliced aromatics (choose 1–3: onion, chives, garlic, shallot, spring onion, leek)

1 cup protein (choose 1–2: grated cheese, chopped cured meats, chopped leftover roast meats or torn smoked salmon or trout), optional

2–3 tsp spices (choose 1–2: ground cumin or coriander, chilli flakes, fennel seeds, dukkah, smoked paprika, or za'atar), optional

1–2 tbsp chopped fresh herbs (choose 1–2: parsley, basil, mint, oregano, thyme), optional

2 eggs or ½ cup mayonnaise

½ cup self-raising flour or plain or chickpea flour mixed with 1 tsp baking powder

cooking oil spray

finishing touches, to serve: fried egg, crispy bacon, sliced avocado, baby spinach leaves, lemon wedges and tomato chutney, optional

Make it

1 Preheat your oven to 180°C fan-forced. Line two baking trays with baking paper.

2 Place your mixed veggies in a large bowl. Stir in your aromatics and your protein, spices and herbs, if using, until everything is combined.

3 In a separate bowl, whisk your eggs or mayonnaise and season with salt and pepper. Add to your veggie mixture and stir well.

4 Add in your flour and gently mix. Test the mixture by pressing a small handful into a fritter. If it doesn't quite hold together add a little more flour, a tablespoon at a time until it does.

5 Scoop ¼ cupfuls of fritter mixture onto prepared trays, leaving a bit of space between them. Spray with olive oil and bake for about 30 minutes, or until golden brown. Alternatively, heat 2–3 tbsp oil in a frying pan; cook ¼ cupfuls of fritter mixture over medium-high heat for 3–4 minutes each side until golden and crisp. Drain on paper towel.

6 Serve fritters for brekkie finished with fried egg, crispy bacon, sliced avocado, spinach leaves, lemon wedges and tomato chutney, if using.

Saveful Tips

Leftover roast veggies work wonders in these fritters: roast pumpkin, potato, cauliflower, sweet potato, beetroot or carrot.

If serving as a snack or in a lunchbox, make a quick and delicious dipping sauce, by mixing some yoghurt with a touch of garlic and cumin.

prep + cook time 35 minutes **serves** 4

French toast

Fluffy, flexible, and irresistible — this dish flips leftover bread (even fruit loaf) into a sweet or savoury showstopper.

Ingredients

4 eggs

1 cup dairy or plant-based liquid (milk, cream, natural yoghurt or sour cream), (see Saveful tips)

1–2 tsp flavour booster (choose 1–2: ground cinnamon, nutmeg, mixed spice, vanilla)

8 slices bread (brioche, sandwich loaf, fruit loaf or croissants)

1–2 tbsp neutral oil or butter

finishing touches, to serve: whipped cream, fresh raspberries, blueberries, halved strawberries and maple syrup, optional

Make it

1 Preheat your oven to 150°C fan-forced.

2 Whisk the eggs, milk (see Saveful tips) and your flavour booster in a large bowl until well combined.

3 Working with a few slices at a time, submerge your bread in the egg mixture until the bread feels wet and saturated but not falling apart. Place bread on a tray then repeat with the remaining slices.

4 Heat a splash of the oil or knob of butter in a frying pan over medium heat. Cook 2 slices of soaked bread, until golden brown, about 2–3 minutes. Flip over and cook the other side for 1–2 minutes, until firm to touch. Place on a baking tray and keep warm in the oven. Repeat in batches with remaining oil or butter and soaked bread.

5 Stack French toast on a plate, finish with a dollop of whipped cream and scatter with mixed berries, then drizzle with maple syrup, if using.

Saveful Tips

No milk? No worries. Use sour cream, or natural or Greek-style yoghurt thinned down with a little water to the consistency of thickened cream.

Lunch

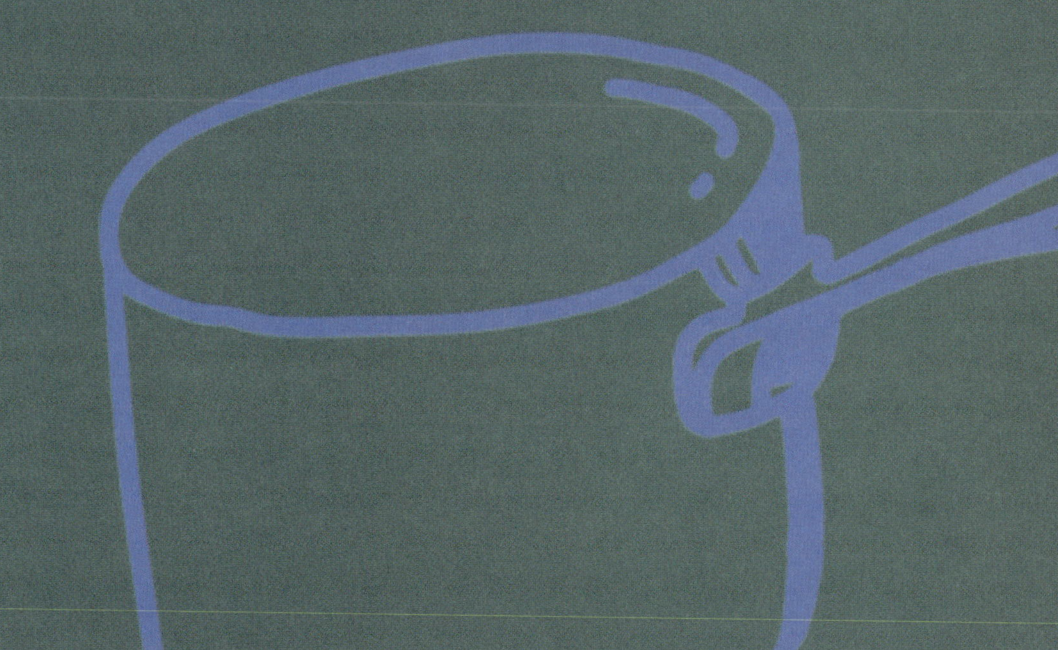

prep + cook time 1 hour 30 minutes **serves** 8

Go-to veggie lasagne

Is there any greater family fave than a lusciously saucy lasagne?

Ingredients

1 quantity veggie bolognese (see recipe page 97)

250g instant dried or fresh lasagne sheets

Cheesy sauce

50g butter or plant-based butter

⅓ cup plain or gluten-free plain flour

1.5 litres (6 cups) dairy or plant-based milk

3 cups grated cheese (choose 1–3: mozzarella, parmesan, cheddar, tasty, Swiss or plant-based)

pinch of nutmeg, optional

Make it

1 Preheat oven to 180°C fan-forced. Heat your bolognese with ¼ cup water in a saucepan over medium heat to loosen.

2 To make the cheesy sauce, melt the butter in a large saucepan over medium-high heat, then stir in the flour. Cook the butter and flour mixture (aka your roux) for 1 minute, stirring, to cook out floury flavour.

3 Add 1 cup of the milk and whisk until smooth. Gradually add the rest of your milk, whisking until silky smooth. Season. Whisk continuously until your sauce is bubbling, about 6–8 minutes. Whisk in 2 cups of the cheese until melted and combined. Check your seasoning and add a pinch of nutmeg, if using.

4 Spread the base of a deep 10cm x 20cm x 25cm ovenproof dish with a little of your bolognese, top with a layer of lasagne sheets, tear or cut to fit the dish. Spread over a thin layer of cheesy sauce, and top with a layer of bolognese about 1cm thick.

5 Continue layering: pasta, then cheese sauce, then bolognese, repeating twice, then finish with a final layer of lasagne sheets and cheese sauce. Scatter with remaining cheese. Ready, steady, bake! Pop into your oven and bake until bubbling and golden brown, 45–55 minutes. Check the doneness by inserting a small knife or skewer into the middle. If it glides in easily, your lasagne is done. Stand for 10 minutes before serving.

STORE Freeze whole unbaked lasagne covered with plastic wrap for up to 3 months.

Saveful tips

Don't have time to make the cheesy sauce? Don't worry, for a quick, lighter and more tangy alternative, mix 5 cups yoghurt with 5 egg yolks, stir in the cheese and season.

prep + cook time 35 minutes **serves** 4

Hearty root veggie soup

Got a couple of carrots, a floppy parsnip or some leftover spuds? This soup turns tired veg into pure comfort in a bowl.

Ingredients

1 tbsp neutral oil or butter

½ cup chopped aromatics (onion, spring onion, leek), optional

4 cups mixed peeled, chopped root veggies (carrot, parsnip, turnip, potato, sweet potato, swede)

1 litre (4 cups) Campbell's Real Stock Vegetable (see Saveful tips)

1–2 tsp flavour boosters (choose 1–2: garlic powder, ground cumin, ground coriander, paprika, chilli, turmeric, curry powder)

2 x 400g can pulses, drained and rinsed (chickpeas, white beans, black beans, mixed beans), optional

1–2 cups chopped green veggies (silverbeet, Brussels sprouts, baby spinach leaves)

finishing touches, to serve: crunchy croûtons, finely grated parmesan and parsley leaves, optional

Make it

1 Heat your oil or butter in a large saucepan over medium-high heat. Add your aromatics, if using; cook until softened, about 5 minutes. Add the root veggies; cook for 5 minutes, stirring occasionally.

2 Pour in your stock. Add your flavour boosters and pulses for extra heartiness and stir well to combine. Bring to a gentle boil, then reduce the heat and simmer for about 20 minutes, until your veggies are tender.

3 Add your chopped green veggies and cook until just wilted, about 5 minutes.

4 Spoon soup into bowls, then finish with crunchy croûtons, grated parmesan and parsley, if using.

STORE Freeze soup in airtight containers for up to 3 months.

Saveful Tips

For a meat lovers version, use Campbell's Real Stock Chicken or Beef and add any leftover chopped roast chicken, lamb, beef or cooked bacon when you add the greens instead of the pulses.

You can blend your soup for a smooth and silky version, or keep it chunky and rustic — it's up to you.

prep + cook time 1 hour 20 minutes **serves** 4

Fridge find falafel

Chickpeas, lentils, leftover veggies — whatever you've got, mix it, shape it, and cook it. Crispy, tasty, fridge-clearing magic.

Ingredients

2 cups falafel base (canned chickpeas, white beans, black beans, or mashed potato, sweet potato or cooked quinoa)

2 cups grated, diced or finely chopped veggies (leftover veggies, grated carrot, grated zucchini) (see Saveful tips)

2 tbsp nuts (choose 1: pine nuts, almonds, macadamias or cashews), optional

½ cup finely chopped aromatics (onion, shallot or leek)

1 tsp flavour booster (choose 1–2: crushed garlic, ground cumin, ground coriander, chilli flakes, za'atar, lemon or lime zest)

1½ cups finely chopped fresh herbs (parsley, coriander, dill, or mint)

2 tbsp lemon or lime juice

1 tsp baking powder

1 egg or ¼ cup mayonnaise

1–2 tbsp plain flour (white, wholemeal, gluten-free or chickpea)

¼ cup neutral oil

finishing touches, to serve: tahini, yoghurt, cos lettuce, cherry tomatoes and lemon wedges, optional

Make it

1 Drain and rinse your chickpeas or beans, if using. Add your chosen base to a blender or food processor. Add in your veggies, and nuts, if using. Next, add your aromatics, flavour booster, herbs and juice.

2 Pulse everything until well combined but still a little chunky; this will help the falafel to hold together and give a crisp shell, you don't want a puree. Transfer to a bowl.

3 Bind it all together by mixing in your baking powder, egg (or mayo), and flour bit by bit until the mixture is soft but doesn't stick to your hands. You want it firm enough to shape, but still soft and moist. Cover and refrigerate for at least 1 hour.

4 Shape your mixture into balls about 5cm in diameter. Heat oil in a large frying pan on medium-high heat; cook falafels, in batches, for about 2 minutes each side until golden. Drain on paper towel. If you prefer to bake your falafel, place them on a lined baking tray, spray with oil and bake in a preheated 200°C fan-forced oven for 15 minutes, turning halfway, until golden and crisp.

5 Serve falafels warm with tahini, yoghurt, cos lettuce, cherry tomatoes and lemon wedges, if you like.

Saveful Tips

Squeeze grated carrot and zucchini in paper towel to remove excess moisture.

If you don't have any baking powder, just swap the plain flour for self-raising flour to keep your falafel light and fluffy.

prep + cook time 30 minutes **serves** 4

Spicy veggie rainbow salad sushi bowl

All the sushi vibes, none of the fuss — fresh, hearty and fridge-friendly.

Ingredients

600g salmon fillets, thickly sliced (see Saveful tips)

flavour booster, to taste (choose 1: chilli powder, curry powder, togarashi spice, garlic powder, onion powder, or paprika), optional

½ cup dressing (thousand island dressing, mayonnaise, or aïoli)

⅓ cup sesame seeds, panko crumbs or crushed nuts

1–1½ cups cooked rice (sushi, shortgrain, brown or jasmine)

6 cups sliced veggies (blanched Asian greens and Brussels sprouts, ribboned zucchini, shredded red cabbage, sliced carrot)

Salad dressing

1 tbsp soy sauce, tamari or sweet chilli sauce

1 tbsp neutral oil

⅓ cup thousand island dressing, mayonnaise or aïoli

¼ cup rice wine or white wine vinegar

squeeze of lime or lemon

finishing touches, to serve: sliced spring onion and pickled red onion, optional

Make it

1 Take your salmon out of the fridge 10 minutes before cooking and season it with salt, pepper and your flavour booster, if using.

2 Place dressing in a shallow dish and sesame seeds in another. Dip each piece of salmon into the dressing, then press into the sesame seeds making sure they are coated evenly.

3 Air fry your salmon at 200°C for 5–7 minutes until golden and crispy (see Saveful tips). If you are using tinned tuna or salmon, skip cooking and flake in later.

4 Meanwhile, to make the salad dressing, whisk the sauce, oil, dressing, and vinegar in a small bowl. Add a squeeze of juice until it tastes balanced.

5 Spoon the rice onto a big platter. Pile your colourful veggies and salmon on top, drizzle with the salad dressing. Finish with spring onion and pickled onion, if using. Serve and enjoy your rainbow bowl of flavour!

Saveful Tips

Swap the salmon for your preferred protein — chicken fillet, beef, lamb, firm white fish, tuna, canned salmon, canned tuna or tofu. If using canned tuna or salmon don't crumb or fry it, just add when assembling.

No air fryer? You can bake your salmon in a preheated 200°C fan-forced oven for 10–12 minutes until it is cooked through.

prep + cook time 30 minutes **serves** 4

Green goddess salad

Fresh, flexible and full of crunch, this green goddess salad is all about using what you've got and dressing it up with herby, zesty magic.

Ingredients

4 cups green goodness (kale, frozen peas, asparagus, broccolini, frozen edamame beans, snow peas)

2 cups extra veggies (cucumber, cabbage, snow pea sprouts, rocket)

2 cups shredded cooked chicken (see Saveful tips)

Green Goddess dressing

1 cup creamy goodness (choose 1–2; honey Dijon mayonnaise, mayonnaise, aïoli, natural or Greek-style yoghurt, sour cream, crème fraîche)

a handful of fresh herbs (choose 1–2: mint, parsley, basil, coriander, dill, or tarragon)

1 tbsp lemon or lime juice, apple cider vinegar, white wine vinegar

flavour boost, to taste (fresh chilli, garlic, honey), optional

1 tbsp olive or avocado oil, optional

finishing touches, to serve:
1 cup mixed toasted nuts & seeds (pistachios, almonds, toasted sunflower seeds, pepitas)

Make it

1 Put your green goodness in a large bowl, pour over boiling water, sit for 5 minutes to soften and brighten. Drain and plunge into cold water to lock in their colour and crunch. Drain again and spread over a large serving plate.

2 Top the blanched greens with your extra veggies and scatter with shredded chicken.

3 To make the green goddess dressing: Add the creamy goodness, fresh herbs, lemon juice, and your flavour booster, if using, to a blender or food processor. Blitz until dressing is smooth and creamy, thinning with a splash of water or oil if needed (see Saveful tips).

4 Pour your dressing generously over the salad and scatter with toasted nuts and seeds. Toss it well so everything is evenly coated and mixed through.

STORE Green Goddess dressing will keep in an airtight container in the fridge for up to 3 days. And trust us, it's the kind of thing you'll want to drizzle on everything.

Saveful Tips

You can swap the chicken for your preferred cooked protein: salmon, beef, lamb, firm white fish, tuna, canned salmon, canned tuna, boiled eggs or tofu.

Taste your dressing and tweak it to your liking. Too zesty? Add a little honey or an extra spoonful of mayo. Not tangy enough? Squeeze in a bit more lemon juice.

prep + cook time 35 minutes **serves** 4

Leftover rice crispy fritters

Leftover rice never tasted this good! Crispy, golden fritters packed with flavour and whatever's in your fridge.

Ingredients

4 cups leftover cooked rice (basmati, jasmine, brown or sushi rice)

2 cups chopped or grated veggies (silverbeet, zucchini, carrot, sweet potato, potato, frozen corn, cabbage)

1–2 tsp flavour booster (choose 1–2: fresh garlic, smoked paprika, ground cumin, ground coriander, garam masala, curry powder, curry paste), optional

1 cup grated cheese (tasty, cheddar, mozzarella or whatever you have)

4 eggs, whisked

¾ cup plain or self-raising flour (spelt, oat, chickpea or wholemeal)

1–1½ cups finely chopped cooked protein (chicken, beef, lamb or ham), optional

½ cup chopped fresh herbs (choose 1–2: parsley, chives, basil, coriander, thyme or oregano), optional

⅓ cup neutral oil

finishing touches, to serve: cucumber salsa, chutney, chilli aïoli and lemon wedges, optional

Make it

1 In a large bowl, add your cooked rice and mix in your veggies and flavour booster, if using. Mix in your cheese which will help bind the fritters together, stir in the eggs.

2 Add the flour, then protein and herbs, if using. Mix all the ingredients until they are just combined. Let the mixture rest for a few minutes.

3 Heat oil in a large, frying pan on medium-high heat. Roll your mixture into small balls and add them, 3 or 4 at a time, to the pan. Flatten down the mixture with a spoon to a fritter shape, being careful not to over crowd your pan.

4 Cook fritters for about 4–5 minutes on each side until they are golden and crunchy. Remove them to a plate lined with paper towel while you cook the remaining fritters.

5 Serve fritters finished with cucumber salsa, chutney, chilli aïoli and lemon wedges, if using.

STORE Fritters can be stored in an airtight container in the fridge for up to 3 days or in the freezer for up to 2 months.

prep + cook time 1 hour **serves** 4

Raid & relish minestrone soup

Minestrone is Italy's ultimate 'big soup' — big on flavour, flexible with ingredients, and always comforting.

Ingredients

2 tbsp neutral oil

2 heaped tbsp butter

½ cup chopped aromatics (choose 1–2: onion, shallots, spring onion, leek)

1–2 tsp dried herbs (choose 1–2: oregano, basil, thyme, sage, rosemary, Italian mixed herbs, chilli flakes)

2–3 cups peeled, chopped hard veggies: (choose 2–3: potato, sweet potato, pumpkin, swede, parsnip, celery, carrots)

1 litre (4 cups) Campbell's Real Stock (Beef, Chicken or Vegetable)

810g canned diced tomatoes

1 cup dried pasta (broken spaghettini or angel hair, or short pasta)

½–1 cup chopped soft veggies (capsicum, green beans, zucchini, peas)

400g can pulses, drained and rinsed (cannellini beans, kidney beans, lentils or chickpeas), optional

1–2 cups chopped leafy greens (kale, baby spinach leaves, silverbeet or beetroot tops), optional

finishing touches, to serve: grated parmesan, chopped parsley and garlic bread, optional

Make it

1 Heat your oil and butter in a large saucepan over medium heat. Add your aromatics and sauté until softened, about 3–4 minutes. Stir in your dried herbs and cook for 1 minute until everything is fragrant.

2 Add your chopped hard vegetables and stir well. Pour in your stock and canned tomatoes, stir everything until it is well combined. Bring to the boil, then reduce the heat to medium-low. Simmer for 15 minutes, until the veggies are almost tender.

3 Stir in the pasta and soft veggies, and pulses, if using, and simmer for 4–5 minutes. Add your leafy greens and cook for a further 2–3 minutes until greens are wilted and pasta is cooked. Season.

4 Ladle soup into bowls, finish with a scattering of parmesan and parsley, and serve with garlic bread, if you like.

Saveful Tips

For the meat lovers, add 1 cup cooked, chopped bacon, chorizo or leftover roast meat instead of the canned pulses.

prep + cook time 45 minutes **serves** 4

Failsafe frittata

Frittata is the ultimate flex. Use up roast veg from last night, scraps of cheese, or herbs on their last legs. It's breakfast, lunch, or dinner sorted in one pan.

Ingredients

1 cup coarsely chopped hardy veg (pumpkin, sweet potato, or potato) (see Saveful tips)

2 tbsp olive oil

½ cup finely chopped aromatics (choose 1–2: onion, spring onion, shallots, leek)

1 cup chopped cured goods (choose 1: pancetta, prosciutto, salami, smoked salmon or trout), optional

½–1 cup sliced tender veggies (kale, silverbeet, zucchini, mushrooms, or asparagus)

1–2 tsp flavour booster (choose 1–2: smoked paprika, ground cumin, za'atar or dukkah)

¼ cup fresh herbs, chopped (oregano, parsley, thyme)

8 eggs

⅓ cup dairy or plant-based milk, optional

1 cup crumbled or grated cheese (haloumi, mozzarella, parmesan)

Make it

1 Preheat your oven to 200°C fan-forced and line a baking tray with baking paper.

2 Spread your hardy veg on the tray, drizzle with some oil, season, and roast about 25 minutes until golden and tender. Remove from oven, reduce your temperature to 180°C.

3 Meanwhile, heat a splash of oil in an ovenproof skillet (25cm–30cm). Add your aromatics; cook about 4–5 minutes until they are soft. Stir in diced cured meat, if using, and cook until lightly browned, about 3–4 minutes. Add in any greens like kale or silverbeet and sauté about 2 minutes until just wilted.

4 Toss in any other tender veggies, smoked fish, if using, and a flavour booster, cook until just softened, about 2 minutes. Add your roasted veggies and stir through your herbs.

5 Whisk the eggs and milk, season well and pour over the veggies and meat. Shake gently so everything settles evenly. Scatter cheese over the top. Bake for 15 minutes, until it is golden and set in the centre. Let it stand for 5–10 minutes before slicing into wedges.

Saveful Tips

No need to peel your pumpkin or potatoes. Just make sure the skin is clean and roast them skin and all!

prep + cook time 50 minutes **serves** 4

Roast chicken & spring veg soup

Got leftover roast chook? Turn it into a flavour-packed soup bursting with spring veggies.

Ingredients

2 tbsp olive oil

1 cup diced aromatics (choose 1–2: onion, spring onions, shallots, leek)

1–2 cups chopped aromatic veggies (choose 1–3: carrot, celery, fennel)

2 cloves garlic, crushed or 1 tsp garlic paste

1.5 litres (6 cups) Campbell's Real Stock (Vegetable or Chicken)

1 cup starch (choose 1–2: chopped potatoes, rice, short pasta, or noodles), optional (see Saveful tips)

4 cups green veggies (choose 2–5: asparagus, broccolini, zucchini, frozen peas, snow peas, sugar snap peas, or baby spinach leaves)

1 cup shredded roast or rotisserie chicken meat (see Saveful tips)

⅓ cup fresh herbs, chopped (basil, mint, oregano, parsley, sage, tarragon), optional

finishing touches, to serve: pesto and finely grated parmesan, optional

Make it

1 Heat oil in a large saucepan over medium-high heat. Add your diced aromatics, chopped aromatic veggies and garlic, with a pinch of salt and sauté for 5–6 minutes, stirring occasionally, until they are tender and translucent.

2 Pour in your stock, season to taste, then bring to a simmer. Let it simmer for about 10 minutes to infuse the flavours.

3 If bulking out your soup, add the starch and stir it well to prevent it sticking; simmer about 10 minutes until your veggies are almost cooked through. Stir in your green veggies and chicken, then cook for 2–3 minutes until veg are bright green and just tender, and chicken is heated through.

4 Boost the flavour with chopped fresh herbs, if using. Check your seasoning.

5 Ladle soup into bowls and finish with a dollop of pesto and a sprinkle of grated parmesan, if using.

Saveful Tips

Use up any leftover cooked noodles, pasta, rice and potatoes, add at the end of step 3 and cook until warmed through.

For extra protein and a heartier soup add drained and rinsed canned cannellini beans or chickpeas.

prep + cook time 1 hour **serves** 4

Mix & match meatloaf

Hearty, budget-friendly, and endlessly adaptable — this meatloaf turns whatever you've got into a family fave.

Ingredients

2 tbsp neutral oil

¾ cup finely diced veggies (carrots, zucchini, celery, potato, sweet potato, capsicum, fennel)

⅓ cup finely diced aromatics (onion, leek, shallots, spring onion)

2–3 tbsp sauce (choose 2–3: Worcestershire sauce, tomato paste, tomato sauce, barbecue sauce or chutney)

1–2 tsp dried herbs (mixed herbs, Italian mixed herbs, oregano, thyme, parsley, rosemary)

1kg mince (beef, chicken, lamb, pork or turkey)

2 eggs or ½ cup mayonnaise

1½ cups dried breadcrumbs or 2 cups fresh

300g rindless bacon rashers

finishing touches, to serve: steamed or roasted vegetables and gravy, optional

Make it

1 Preheat your oven to 180°C fan-forced and grease a 10cm x 20cm loaf tin.

2 Heat oil in a large frying pan on medium heat, add veggies, aromatics, sauce and dried herbs. Cook for about 5 minutes until they are softened and fragrant. Transfer to a large bowl and allow to cool slightly.

3 Add mince to your cooled vegetables and mix to combine. Add your eggs and breadcrumbs and mix thoroughly until everything is well combined. Season.

4 Line your loaf tin with the rindless bacon, allowing strips to hang over the edges. Press the meatloaf mixture firmly into the tin and fold the bacon strips over the top to cover the mixture. Cover your meatloaf with foil and bake for 1 hour. Remove the foil for the last 10 minutes to allow the top to crisp and turn golden.

5 Let your meatloaf rest in the tin for about 10 minutes before serving. Carefully flip onto a platter. Serve thick slices with steamed or roasted vegetables and gravy, if you like.

STORE Wrap meatloaf whole or in slices in plastic wrap and freeze for up to 3 months.

Don't have enough of one kind of mince? Mix it up! Combine beef with pork, chicken with lentils, or you can even use sausages — just squeeze the meat out of their casings and mix them in.

Pickled mixed veggies

Pack 2 cups small cauliflower florets, 1 cup sliced carrot, ½ cup sliced capsicum and ½ cup sliced zucchini tightly into 3 or 4 sterilised jars. Add 1 bay leaf and 1 tsp peppercorns to each jar. Cover with hot pickling liquid.

Pickling liquid

prep + cook time 30 minutes

Combine 2 cups water, ¾ cup vinegar (apple cider, white vinegar or white wine) with 2–4 tbsp sweetener (white sugar, raw sugar, honey or maple syrup) to taste in a saucepan. Add 1 tbsp salt. Bring the mixture to a simmer over a high heat. Carefully pour enough hot liquid over your jars of packed veggies to submerge. Seal.

tips Got forgotten veggies? Pickle them tender! Crunchy, tangy, and perfect for perking up sandwiches, salads, or snack time. Pickles will keep in the fridge for up to 1 month.

Chilli cucumber pickles

Pack 4 cups sliced cucumber tightly into 3 or 4 sterilised jars. Add 1 tsp each chopped fresh chilli and mustard seeds, and 1 garlic clove to each jar. Cover with hot pickling liquid.

Zucchini & dill pickles

Pack 4 cups sliced zucchini tightly into 3 or 4 sterilised jars. Add 1 tsp mustard seeds and 1 tsp dill seeds to each jar. Cover with hot pickling liquid.

Pickled red onion

Pack 4 cups sliced red onion tightly into 3 or 4 sterilised jars. Add 1 tsp each mustard seeds, black peppercorns and coriander seeds to each jar. Cover with hot pickling liquid.

prep + cook time 40 minutes **serves** 4

Vego burger

These patties are made for swapping and riffing with whatever's on hand.

Ingredients

1 tbsp neutral oil

½ cup finely diced aromatics (choose 2–3: onion, shallots, leek, fresh ginger, garlic cloves)

2 cups cooked chopped veggies (carrots, potatoes, mushrooms, broccoli, beetroot, cauliflower, frozen mixed veg, kale, spinach, pumpkin, sweet potato, zucchini)

½ cup dried or panko breadcrumbs, polenta or rolled oats

1 cup cooked grains (rice, barley, quinoa, burghul), optional

400g can pulses, drained and rinsed (beans, chickpeas, lentils), optional

1–2 tsp ground spices (choose 1–2: cumin, coriander, paprika, chilli), optional

2–3 tbsp finely chopped fresh herbs (choose 1–2: parsley, coriander, dill, mint, lemongrass, rosemary or thyme), optional

finely grated rind and juice of ½ lemon, optional

½ cup grated cheese (cheddar, feta or haloumi)

4 brioche or burger buns, halved and toasted

finishing touches, to serve: mayonnaise, lettuce leaves, tomato sauce, sliced red onion, and mint leaves

Make it

1 Preheat your oven to 200°C fan-forced. Line a baking tray with baking paper.

2 Heat your oil in a small frying pan over medium heat, sauté your aromatics until soft, about for 3–4 minutes.

3 In a food processor, add your sautéed aromatics, cooked veggies, and breadcrumbs. Then add your grains, pulses, spices, herbs and lemon, if using. Pulse until the mixture is combined but still has texture. Transfer to a bowl. Press a little mixture between fingers, if it holds together, continue. If it is too dry add a little water, 1 tbsp at a time; if it is too wet, add more breadcrumbs. Stir in your grated cheese.

4 Divide the mixture into 4, and using damp hands shape into patties and place on the lined baking tray. Brush them with a little more oil and bake for 10–15 minutes until they are golden and cooked.

5 Spread warm toasted bun bases with mayonnaise, top with lettuce, a patty, a drizzle of sauce, sliced onion and mint leaves. Crown with the bun top and serve!

STORE Make a double batch of patties then freeze the leftover cooked patties for up to 3 months.

Saveful Tips

Add extra fillings to your burger such as avocado, spinach, beetroot, canned pineapple, tomatoes, cucumber and your favourite pickle.

No buns in the pantry? No excuse — you can use lettuce leaves for a carb-free option!

prep + cook time 1 hour **serves** 4

Warm Asian-inspired salad

Roasty, toasty and satisfying, this warm veg and grain salad is hearty enough for lunch and flexible enough to use whatever you've got.

Ingredients

1 cup uncooked rice (brown, wild, basmati or jasmine)

1–2 tbsp neutral oil

2–3 cups veggies, cut into florets, chunks or wedges (cauliflower, pumpkin, sweet potato, and fennel)

1 cup leafy greens (choose 1–3: sliced kale, baby spinach leaves, rocket, mixed salad leaves) (see Saveful tips)

4 soft boiled eggs (see Saveful tips)

½ cup crunch (choose 1–3: smoked or natural almonds, toasted pumpkin seeds, toasted sunflower seeds)

Dressing

1 tbsp neutral oil

1 tbsp sesame oil (or extra neutral oil), to taste

2 tbsp vinegar (rice wine, brown rice or black vinegar), to taste

1 tbsp soy sauce (soy, mushroom soy or tamari), to taste

2 tsp toasted sesame seeds

2–3 tsps flavour booster (choose 1–3: miso paste, mirin, honey chilli paste, chilli oil or sauce, fresh or pickled ginger, crushed garlic cloves or paste), optional

finishing touches, to serve: coriander leaves

Make it

1 Preheat your oven to 200°C fan-forced. Line baking trays with baking paper. Bring a saucepan of water to the boil. Cook your rice according to the packet instructions. Drain and set aside.

2 Drizzle your veggies with oil, toss to coat, season to taste and spread on baking trays. Roast for 30–35 minutes until tender and caramelised. Stand for 5 minutes then transfer to a serving bowl.

3 To make the dressing, combine the oils, vinegar, soy sauce and sesame seeds in a screw-top jar. If you want more flavour, add flavour booster: a little umami (miso), sweetness (mirin or honey), heat (a hint of chilli) and aroma (ginger and garlic).

4 Combine leafy greens, rice and roasted veggies on a large serving platter or bowl. Top with torn eggs, and scatter over your crunch elements.

5 Shake your dressing well and drizzle over the salad just before serving, season to taste and toss to combine. Finish with a scattering of coriander leaves.

Saveful Tips

If using kale, remove tough stems then combine in a bowl with a splash of oil and a squeeze of lemon; rub with your hands to soften the leaves.

Swap boiled eggs for any leftover protein you may have in the fridge such as barbecued or roasted chicken, steak, lamb, sausages or pork.

prep + cook time 45 minutes **serves** 4

Grandma's rissoles

Channel Grandma's wisdom and roll up a batch or two of rissoles. Simple, satisfying, and perfect for using up odds and ends.

Ingredients

1–2 tbsp neutral oil

½ cup chopped aromatics (onion, shallots, spring onion, leek, celery, fennel)

1–2 tsp flavour booster (choose 1–2: garlic powder, ground chilli, cumin, coriander, paprika, curry powder)

⅓ cup cured meat (chopped bacon, ham or salami), optional

½ cup dried breadcrumbs or panko crumbs or 1 cup fresh breadcrumbs

1–2 cups grated veggies (zucchini, potato, pumpkin, sweet potato, frozen peas, frozen corn kernels) (see Saveful tips)

500g mince (beef, chicken, turkey, pork or plant-based)

1 egg, whisked or ¼ cup mayonnaise

1–2 tsp dried herbs (choose 1–2: thyme, Italian mixed herbs, oregano, parsley, rosemary), optional

2 tbsp sauce (Worcestershire, tomato, barbecue or chutney)

1 tbsp neutral oil

Make it

1 Heat the oil in a frying pan on a medium heat and sauté your aromatics for 3–4 minutes until soft and fragrant. Stir in your flavour booster and cured meat, if using, and cook for another 2 minutes.

2 Stir in the breadcrumbs, cooking for 1 minute to soak up the flavours. Stir in your veggies and cook briefly to combine. Transfer to a bowl. Stand for 5 minutes.

3 Add your mince to the bowl and mix until everything is well combined. Add your egg, dried herbs and sauce, if using, and mix everything together until it is well combined. Roll ¼-cupfuls of your mixture into patties.

4 Heat oil in a large frying pan on medium-high heat; cook rissoles for 3–4 minutes on each side until they are golden and cooked through. Alternatively, to bake your rissoles, place them on a baking tray lined with baking paper, and bake in a preheated 200°C fan-forced oven for 15 minutes. Flip over and bake for another 10 minutes until golden.

STORE Freeze uncooked rissoles wrapped in plastic wrap for up to 3 months.

Saveful Tips

Swap 1 cup veggies with 1 cup drained, rinsed canned cannellini beans, kidney beans, lentils or chickpeas for extra protein.

Turn your rissoles into a tasty rissole parmigiana, perfect for dinner — just top with pasta sauce and cheese, then bake until cheese melts.

prep + cook time 40 minutes **serves** 4

Mediterranean grain salad

This grain-based dish ticks all the boxes: hearty, thrifty and ready to pair with whatever's in your fridge.

Ingredients

1 cup uncooked grains (barley, rice, buckwheat, burghul, farro, freekeh or quinoa) (see Saveful tips)

2 cups veggies (blanched fresh or frozen corn kernels, halved cherry or medley tomatoes, blanched or roasted cauliflower, spinach leaves)

½ cup citrus segments (blood orange, ruby grapefruit, grapefruit), optional

2–3 tbsp sweet and sour (choose 1–2: dried fruit (sweet): apricot, raisins, cranberries, sultanas; or pickled veg (sour): cornichons, onion, ginger, chillies), optional

1 cup protein (drained and rinsed tinned black beans, kidney beans, chickpeas or lentils, or leftover chopped roast pork or turkey)

½ cup fresh herbs, leaves picked (mint, coriander, basil or parsley)

⅓–½ cup crumbled or grated cheese (feta, bocconcini, ricotta, blue cheese or parmesan)

Dressing

½–⅔ cup olive oil, to taste

¼–⅓ cup lemon juice or white-wine vinegar, to taste

flavour booster (1 clove garlic, crushed, 1 tsp finely grated lemon rind), optional

finishing touches, to serve: chopped natural almonds and sunflower seeds

Make it

1 Boil a saucepan of salted water, add your grains and cook following packet instructions until just tender. Drain and rinse under cold water, shake well to get rid of excess water. Set aside.

2 To make dressing: Add all your dressing ingredients to a screw-top jar or leak-proof container. Season with salt and pepper, then shake well to combine. Taste and adjust to your liking, add more oil if it is too acidic, or more lemon/vinegar if it needs extra punch. Set aside.

3 Combine vegetables and citrus, if using, in a large bowl. The citrus will add an extra dimension to the flavour of the salad. Add your dried fruit and/or pickled veg, if using. Stir in your cooled grains and mix gently. Add your protein and half the herbs, if using, then gently combine everything together.

4 Pour over your dressing and toss until evenly coated.

5 Scatter cheese and remaining herbs over, then finish with a scattering of chopped almonds and sunflower seeds.

Saveful tips

Use up whatever leftover cooked rice or grains, or a combination of up to three varieties, you have in your fridge; you'll need about 2–3 cups in total.

This recipe is perfect to use up seasonal ingredients:
Autumn/Winter **cauliflower, citrus, carrot, fennel;**
Spring **asparagus, snow peas, sugar snap peas, zucchini;**
Summer **cucumber, tomatoes, radishes.**

Dinner

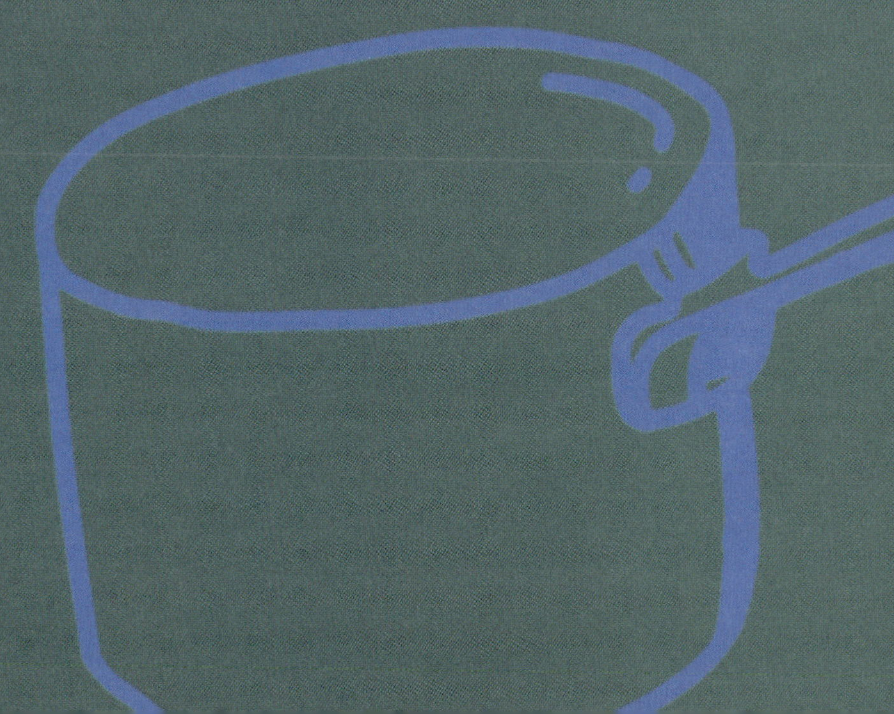

prep + cook time 45 minutes + marinating **serves** 4

Tex-Mex one pan

One pan, endless possibilities! This Tex-Mex flex is zesty, hearty, and perfect for tossing in whatever you've got!

Ingredients

- 4 garlic cloves, crushed or 4 tsp garlic paste
- 2 tsp each smoked paprika, coriander and cumin powder
- 1½ tsp each salt and pepper
- ¼ cup olive oil
- 1 tbsp lime or lemon juice
- 4 chicken thighs and 4 drumsticks
- ½ cup chopped aromatics (choose 1–2: onion, shallot, spring onion, leek)
- 2 cups mixed chopped veggies (choose 1–4: capsicum, peas, corn, zucchini, broccoli)
- 1 cup uncooked medium-grain rice
- 1 cup Campbell's Real Stock (Chicken or Vegetable) or water
- ¾ cup crushed or diced canned tomatoes
- 400g can black beans or kidney beans, drained and rinsed
- finishing touches, to serve: chopped coriander, sliced avocado, sliced jalapeño, lime wedges and sour cream, optional

Make it

1 Preheat the oven to 180°C fan-forced.

2 In a large bowl, mix half the garlic, the spices, salt and pepper, 1 tbsp olive oil and the lime juice to form a paste. Add your chicken and toss to coat evenly with the paste. Cover and marinate in the fridge for at least 1 hour or overnight.

3 Heat 1 tbsp oil in a large, deep ovenproof frying pan on a medium-high heat. Place the marinated chicken, skin-side down, in the pan and sear for 4 minutes or until lightly golden. Flip them over and cook a further 1½ minutes. Transfer to a plate. Clean pan of burnt spices if necessary.

4 Heat remaining oil in the same pan, sauté your aromatics and remaining garlic until just softened, about 3 minutes. Add your veggies and sauté until veggies are softened, about 3 minutes.

5 Stir in your rice to coat in oil, then add the stock, tomatoes and beans. Stir well to combine everything. Nestle the seared chicken on top of the rice, skin-side up and bring the mixture to a simmer. Cover your pan with a lid or foil and bake in the oven for about 25 minutes.

6 Remove cover and bake a further 15 minutes, until only small pockets of liquid remain on the rice's surface. Remove from oven and rest uncovered for about 10 minutes until liquid is fully absorbed. Drizzle with lime juice and fluff the rice around the chicken. Finish with a scattering of coriander, sliced avocado, sliced jalapeños, lime wedges, and sour cream on the side.

Saveful Tips

Don't have the individual spices? No worries, substitute the spices with a sachet of taco, burrito or fajita seasoning.

prep + cook time 40 minutes **serves** 4

Old-fashioned leftover roast curry

This old-school curry takes whatever meat (and veg) you've got and transforms it into a rich, hearty bowl of nostalgia.

Ingredients

¼ cup neutral oil

½ cup mixed chopped aromatics (choose 1–2: onion, leek, shallot, spring onion)

2–3 tbsp curry powder or curry paste

3 tsp flavour booster (choose 2–3: crushed garlic or garlic paste, grated ginger or ginger paste, turmeric powder, ground cumin, coriander, or chilli)

½ cup chopped hard veggies (choose 1–3: carrot, parsnip, potato, pumpkin)

2 tbsp plain or self-raising flour

3 cups Campbell's Real Stock (Beef, Chicken or Vegetable)

½ cup tomato (diced fresh or canned, chutney, or passata)

½ cup dairy or plant-based liquid (cream, milk, sour cream, coconut cream, Greek-style yoghurt)

2–2½ cups leftover roast beef, cut into 2cm pieces (see Saveful tips)

½ cup tender veggies (peas, beans, frozen mixed veg)

finishing touches, to serve: toasted flaked almonds, coriander leaves, yoghurt and naan, optional

Make it

1 Heat your oil in a large saucepan over a medium heat then add your aromatics and cook for 1–2 minutes until softened. Stir in your curry powder or paste and flavour boosters, then cook for 1–2 minutes, until fragrant.

2 Add in your hard vegetables and sauté for 3–4 minutes, stirring occasionally. Sprinkle in the flour and gradually pour in the stock, stirring well to avoid any lumps. Simmer for 5 minutes until your sauce is slightly thickened.

3 Next, stir in your tomatoes and liquid. Add your roast beef, stirring until everything is well combined. Bring to the boil, then reduce heat and simmer gently for 15 minutes, stirring occasionally. Add your tender veggies, cook for 5–10 minutes stirring occasionally, until the vegetables are tender and the curry is rich and flavourful.

4 Finish your curry with a scattering of toasted almonds and coriander leaves with naan on the side, if you like.

Saveful Tips

This curry works with just about any leftover roast meat, such as roast lamb, chicken, turkey or even pork. Bulk it out with chickpeas, lentils or extra veggies.

Just like Mum or Nan used to do, add a handful of chopped apple, sultanas, or dried apricots to your curry. A touch of fruity sweetness takes this curry to comforting new heights, and clears out your fruit bowl and pantry too!

prep + cook time 40 minutes **serves** 4

Hug-in-a-crust pot pies

These pot pies are the ultimate in comfort food — golden, hearty and endlessly flexible. Perfect for turning leftover roast meats or veggies into a brand-new, weeknight win.

Ingredients

2 tbsp neutral oil

½ cup mixed finely sliced aromatics (choose 1–2: onion, shallots, spring onion, chives, leek)

1–2 cloves garlic or 1 tsp garlic powder, optional

1 cup chopped mixed veggies (cauliflower, zucchini, carrots, mushrooms, celery, or potato)

2 cups chopped leftover cooked meat (chicken, lamb, beef, or pork)

½ cup extra protein (chopped bacon, canned lentils or chickpeas)

1 cup Campbell's Real Stock (Chicken, Beef or Vegetable) or water

1 cup dairy or plant-based liquid (milk, cream, sour cream, crème fraîche or evaporated milk)

2 tbsp finely chopped fresh herbs (parsley, thyme), optional

2–3 sheets frozen puff or shortcrust pastry, just thawed

1 whisked egg or 2 tbsp milk, for brushing

Make it

1 Preheat your oven to 200°C fan-forced. Grease 4 x 1-cup oven-safe ramekins or 1 large pie dish.

2 Heat oil in a large frying pan on medium heat then add your aromatics and garlic. Cook until they are softened, about 5 minutes. Stir in your mixed veggies and cook for another 2–3 minutes until they are tender.

3 Mix through your leftover meat and extra protein, if using, until everything is combined.

4 Next, add your stock and liquid to the pan, then stir in your herbs, if using. Bring the mixture to the boil, then reduce the heat and simmer for about 5 minutes until it has thickened. Spoon the mixture evenly into your prepared ramekins or pie dish.

5 Cut your pastry slightly larger than the ramekins or pie dish and lay over the top, tucking in edges. Brush your pies with the beaten egg or milk then poke a small sharp knife in each to release steam.

6 Bake pies for about 20 minutes, or until the pastry is golden, puffed, and irresistible! Cool them slightly before serving.

Saveful Tips

Use fresh veg, frozen veg or leftover cooked veg for these pies. Whatever you have in the fridge: peas, beans, broccoli, potato, pumpkin, corn, or leftover cooked veggies will work.

prep + cook time 45 minutes **serves** 4

Don't wait for Friday fish

Takeaway vibes without leaving home — this is fish & chips your way.

Ingredients

750g firm white fish fillets (flathead, barramundi, basa, frozen fish fillets)

½ cup rice flour

2 cups neutral oil, approximately, for frying

Batter

1 cup self-raising flour (or 1 cup plain flour + 1½ tsp baking powder)

½ cup cornflour (or arrowroot, tapioca or potato flour)

1–2 tsp ground spices (choose 1–2: smoked paprika, chilli powder, cumin, garam masala), optional

1 cup chilled sparkling liquid (beer, soda water or mineral water)

finishing touches, to serve: hot chips, tartare sauce and lemon wedges, optional

Make it

1 Preheat oven to 100°C fan-forced.

2 Pat your fish fillets dry with paper towel and cut into 5cm thick strips. Season generously with salt and pepper and lightly coat each piece in rice flour, shaking off any excess flour.

3 Heat enough oil in a large deep saucepan to submerge the fish. Heat to 190°C (or test the temperature with a small piece of bread; it should sizzle and turn golden in about 30 seconds).

4 Meanwhile, make the batter: In a large bowl, whisk together your flour, cornflour and spices, if using. Gradually whisk in the chilled sparkling liquid until you have a smooth and slightly thick batter.

5 Dip fish pieces one at a time into the batter, coating them completely. Fry 2–3 pieces at a time for about 5–7 minutes, turning occasionally, until golden and crisp. Drain the fish on a paper-towel-lined baking tray. Keep warm in the oven while you repeat with the remaining fish and batter.

6 Serve battered fish with hot chips, tartare sauce and lemon wedges, if using.

Saveful Tips

Not into fish? No worries — you can make a delicious veggie version too! Cut eggplant, zucchini, sweet potato or pumpkin into 1cm thick slices and prepare as per the fish.

prep + cook time 45 minutes **serves** 4

One tray tandoori

Turn dinner into a flavour-packed feast with this easy tandoori tray-bake. It's big on flavour, low on fuss, and guaranteed to please!

Ingredients

¾ cup yoghurt (Greek-style, natural or coconut)

2–3 tbsp tandoori paste

1–2 tbsp lemon or lime juice

1–2 cloves crushed garlic or 1 tsp garlic paste

1–2 tsp grated fresh ginger or 1 tsp ginger paste

300g cauliflower (cut into large florets)

300g sweet potato or potato, cut into thick wedges

1 red onion, cut into thick wedges

1 tbsp neutral oil

500g firm tofu, drained, thickly sliced

a large handful of fresh green beans, trimmed

finishing touches, to serve: steamed rice, roti, mint yoghurt, lime halves, fresh mint and coriander leaves, optional

Make it

1 Preheat oven to 200°C fan-forced. Line two baking trays with baking paper.

2 Stir the yoghurt, tandoori paste, juice, garlic and ginger in a large bowl to combine. Toss cauliflower, sweet potato and onion in the marinade to coat well. Spread evenly on the lined trays, shaking off any excess marinade back into your bowl.

3 Drizzle a little oil over your veggies and pop them in the oven to roast until semi-tender, about 15 minutes.

4 Add tofu to remaining marinade and toss to coat well. Place on top of veggies. Toss beans in a little oil, place on tray. Roast until tofu is lightly charred, about 10–15 minutes.

5 Serve tandoori with steamed rice, roti, mint yoghurt, lime halves, and a scattering of fresh mint and coriander.

Saveful Tips

Allow about 150–250g of raw vegetables per person and 150–180g of protein per person. Substitute tofu with chicken breast, lamb cutlets, lamb backstrap, sirloin steak or fresh salmon fillets, the cooking time may need to be adjusted.

Choose large, low-sided baking trays, to help hot air circulate easily around the ingredients for maximum browning and caramelisation and therefore, max flavour! Beware of overcrowding. If necessary, spread your ingredients across mulitple smaller trays.

Saveful Tips

Meatballs are a great recipe to get the kids involved in — little hands are perfect for mixing the meatball mixture and rolling the meatballs.

Leftover makeover: Turn your leftover meatballs into meatball subs or spoon over the top of a pizza and finish with your favourite toppings.

prep + cook time 1 hour 30 minutes **serves** 4

Baked meatballs

There's a lot to love about tender meatballs simmered in a rich tomato sauce — so much flavour and so much possibility for riffs and variations.

Ingredients

1 large onion

1 tbsp olive oil

3–4 cloves crushed garlic or 2 tsp garlic paste

½ cup finely chopped fennel or celery, optional

800g can diced or cherry tomatoes

1 flavour booster (1–2 bay leaves, sprig of fresh thyme, ½ tsp chilli flakes)

1 cup liquid flavour (Campbell's Real Stock Beef, Chicken or Vegetable, or red or white wine)

½ cup breadcrumbs (fresh, dried, panko, or rolled oats)

500g mince (beef, pork or chicken)

1 cup extra veggies (grated carrot or zucchini, diced broccoli or mushrooms)

1 egg, whisked

½ cup finely grated cheese (parmesan, tasty or cheddar), optional

1–2 tsp dried herbs (choose 2–3: rosemary, thyme, sage, mixed Italian herbs, or fennel seeds), optional

2 cups baby spinach leaves or chopped silverbeet

finishing touches, to serve: finely grated parmesan and long pasta

Make it

1 Preheat your oven to 220°C fan-forced. Lightly oil a 25cm x 30cm roasting pan (or 25cm–30cm shallow ovenproof casserole dish).

2 Grate your onion over a small bowl to catch all the juice. Heat oil in a large saucepan on medium-high heat. Add half the grated onion and half your garlic along with the fennel or celery, if using. Sauté until softened, about for 4–5 minutes.

3 Stir in your canned tomatoes, flavour booster, and liquid flavour. Season and simmer for 20 minutes, until it is rich and slightly thickened.

4 In a large bowl, mix your remaining onion and garlic with the breadcrumbs, stand for 5 minutes to soften; add a splash of milk or water if breadcrumbs are too dry. Add your mince, veggies and egg. Add the cheese and dried herbs, if using, season well and mix thoroughly to combine until it is sticky.

5 Roll 2 tablespoons of mixture into balls, place them in the oiled roasting pan or casserole dish, and drizzle or spray them with a little more oil. Bake for about 10 minutes, shaking the pan occasionally, until they are browned. Reduce oven temperature to 160°C fan-forced. (Keep door ajar to reduce the temp quickly.)

6 Pour your sauce over browned meatballs, turning to coat each meatball in sauce. Bake for a further 25–30 minutes, until meatballs are cooked through and the sauce is thick and rich. Add spinach or silverbeet and stir gently until wilted.

7 Finish meatballs with a scattering of finely grated parmesan and serve tossed through your favourite long pasta.

STORE Freeze leftover meatballs in an airtight container for up to 6 months.

prep + cook time 45 minutes **serves** 4

Roast chicken enchiladas

From roast chook to crowd-pleaser — saucy, cheesy, and bubbling with flavour.

Ingredients

3 tbsp olive oil

½ cup finely diced aromatics (choose 1–2: onion, shallots, spring onion)

2 cloves garlic, crushed or 1 tsp garlic paste

2 cups veggies (chopped capsicum, corn kernels, baby spinach leaves, grated carrot, or grated zucchini)

1½ cups coarsely chopped leftover cooked chicken or rotisserie chicken

2 cups leftover cooked rice

400g can black or kidney beans, drained and rinsed, optional

10 x 20cm flour tortillas

1¼ cups grated cheese (cheddar, mozzarella or Swiss)

Spice mix

1 tbsp ground cumin

1 tbsp paprika or smoked paprika

1 tbsp fresh or dried oregano

1–2 tsp chilli powder or chilli flakes, optional, to taste

1 tsp ground coriander

2 tsp onion or garlic powder

Sauce

2 tbsp plain or gluten-free plain flour

2 cups Campbell's Real Stock (Chicken or Vegetable)

400g can diced tomatoes or 375ml passata

1–2 tsp chipotle chilli in adobo or hot sauce, to taste, optional

finishing touches, to serve: sour cream, chunky guacamole, fresh coriander leaves, and lime wedges, optional

Make it

1 Preheat the oven to 180°C fan-forced. Lightly oil a 25cm x 35cm rectangular baking dish.

2 To make spice mix: Combine all the spices in a small bowl. Add 1 tsp salt and 1 tsp ground black pepper, mix well.

3 To make the sauce: Heat 2 tbsp of the oil in a saucepan over medium-high heat, add the flour and cook, stirring continuously, for 1 minute. Stir in 2 tbsp of your spice mix and cook, stirring for another 30 seconds until fragrant and grainy. Gradually pour in the stock, whisking until combined and smooth. Add tomatoes and chilli in adobo or hot sauce, if using. Season to taste and simmer for 2–3 minutes until thickened. Set aside.

4 Heat remaining 1 tbsp oil in a large frying pan over medium-high heat; add the aromatics and garlic, and sauté until softened, about 5 minutes. Add your veggies to the pan and sauté for about 5–6 minutes until just tender. (If using baby spinach, add at the very end of cooking to just wilt.) Season to taste and remove from the heat.

5 Add chicken, rice and beans, if using, to the pan. Add your remaining spice mix and mix well. If your filling is dry, add about ¼ cup water to moisten it.

6 Spread 1 cup sauce over base of baking dish. Spoon a heaped ½ cup of filling along the bottom third of each tortilla and scatter with a little cheese. Roll to enclose the filling and place seam-side down in the baking dish. Spoon over the remaining sauce. Sprinkle with remaining cheese.

7 Pop your enchiladas into the oven and bake until bubbling and golden brown, about 25–30 minutes should do it! Finish it topped with sour cream, chunky guacamole and coriander leaves, with lime wedges on the side, if using.

STORE Freeze enchiladas in an airtight container for up to 2 months.

prep + cook time 8 hours 30 minutes **serves** 4

Slow cooker braised chicken

Slow-cooked, saucy, and oh-so-juicy. This foolproof chicken dish turns budget cuts into melt-in-your-mouth deliciousness.

Ingredients

splash of neutral oil

2 carrots, chopped

2 cups diced aromatics (choose 1–2: onion, shallots, leek)

3–4 garlic cloves, crushed or 2–3 tsp garlic paste

1 tbsp spices (choose 1–2: ground cumin, chilli flakes, paprika or smoked paprika)

1–2 tbsp fresh herbs (choose 1–2: oregano, bay leaves, thyme, rosemary)

1.5kg chicken drumsticks, thigh cutlets or marylands

400g can diced or cherry tomatoes

400ml liquid (choose 2: Campbell's Real Stock Chicken or Vegetable, sour cream or cream)

1–2 cups chopped extra veg (choose 2–3: frozen peas, eggplant, baby spinach, kale or silverbeet)

2–3 tsp lemon juice or white vinegar, optional

finishing touches, to serve: mash and oregano leaves, optional

Make it

1 Heat a splash of oil in a large frying pan over medium-high heat or use the sauté function on your slow cooker if available. Add your carrots and aromatics. Cook, stirring occasionally until lightly browned, about 6–8 minutes. Season, then stir in your garlic, spices and herbs, cook for a further 1–2 minutes. Transfer to your slow cooker if necessary and turn heat to low.

2 Heat a splash of oil in a clean frying pan over medium-high heat. Pat your chicken dry with paper towel; season generously. Sear chicken, in batches, on all sides until browned, transferring to the slow cooker after each batch. Add ½ cup water to the pan to deglaze, scraping up the caramelised bits; pour everything into the slow cooker.

3 Add tomatoes and liquid mixture to slow cooker. Season to taste. Cover and cook on low for 8 hours, until the meat is tender and falling apart. In the last 15 minutes, stir in extra veggies and juice or vinegar, if using.

4 Remove the chicken from the slow cooker. Simmer the sauce uncovered for 10–15 minutes to thicken. Pull chicken into chunks then return to the sauce. Adjust seasoning.

5 Serve braised chicken on mash, scattered with oregano leaves, if using.

STORE Freeze chicken braise in an airtight container for up to 3 months.

No slow-cooker? No worries. You can make this in an ovenproof casserole or baking dish. Add 1½ cups of extra water or stock, bring to a simmer on the stove, then transfer your covered dish to a low oven (150°C fan-forced) and bake 4–5 hours until chicken falls apart. Reduce sauce on the stove top if needed.

Indian-style pumpkin soup

Heat 1 tbsp neutral oil in a large saucepan, add 2 tbsp of your favourite Indian-style curry paste or powder, 2 tsp ginger paste and a pinch of chilli flakes, if you like. Continue as per the soup base below and blend. Substitute the milk with 1 cup natural or coconut yoghurt; thin with extra Campbell's Real Stock, if you like. Serve with a dollop of yoghurt, topped with spiced pepitas and mint sprigs.

Classic pumpkin soup base

prep + cook time 30 minutes **serves** 4

Combine 1.2kg chopped, peeled pumpkin or a mix of pumpkin, potato and sweet potato in a large saucepan with 1 chopped onion and 2 cloves crushed garlic. Cover with 1 litre (4 cups) Campbell's Real Stock (Vegetable or Chicken), season. Bring to the boil over high heat, then simmer for 15 minutes until veggies are very tender. Use a stick blender to puree. Return to medium heat, then add ¾ cup dairy or plant-based milk, cream or sour cream and blend until smooth.

Thai-style pumpkin soup

Heat 1 tbsp neutral oil in a large saucepan, add 2 tbsp of your favourite Thai curry paste, 2 tsp grated ginger and 1 tsp lemongrass paste, optional. Continue as per the soup base opposite and blend. Substitute the milk with 270ml coconut cream or coconut milk, season; thin with extra Campbell's Real Stock, if you like. Serve with a drizzle of coconut cream, chopped roasted peanuts, fried shallots, sliced red chilli, and coriander sprigs.

Bacon & corn-style pumpkin soup

Heat 1 tbsp oil in a large saucepan, cook 4 rashers chopped streaky bacon until golden. Remove bacon with a slotted spoon. Continue as per the soup base opposite, adding 1 cup fresh or frozen corn kernels and half the cooked bacon with the pumpkin. Blend, then add milk or cream of choice. Serve with a drizzle of cream, scatter with chopped parsley, remaining bacon and a few blanched corn kernels.

prep + cook time 8 hours 30 minutes **serves** 4

Slow cooker tomato-y meat ragu

This set-and-forget ragu turns everyday ingredients into a flavour-packed feast.

Ingredients

splash of olive oil

2 carrots, chopped

1½ cup diced aromatics (onion, shallots, leek)

¾ cup diced celery or fennel, optional

3–4 garlic cloves, crushed or 3 tsp garlic paste

3 tsp chopped fresh herbs (choose 1–2: sage, thyme, oregano, tarragon or rosemary)

1.2kg stewing meat cut into 4 large pieces (see Saveful tips)

½–¾ cup wine (red, rosé or white) or water, optional

400g can diced or cherry tomatoes

400ml Campbell's Real Stock (Beef or Vegetable)

1–2 cups tender veggies (choose 1–3: mushrooms, zucchini, kale, silverbeet, baby spinach), optional

finishing touches, to serve: pappardelle, fresh thyme and oregano leaves, finely grated parmesan, optional

Make it

1 Heat a splash of oil in a large frying pan over medium-high heat or use the sauté function on your slow cooker if available.

2 Add your carrots, aromatics and celery or fennel. Cook, stirring occasionally until lightly browned, about 6–8 minutes. Season, then stir in your garlic and herbs, cook for another 1–2 minutes. Transfer to your slow cooker if necessary and turn heat to low.

3 Heat a splash of oil in a clean frying pan over medium-high heat. Pat your meat dry with paper towel, season generously. Sear beef, in batches, on all sides until browned, transferring to the slow cooker after each batch. Add wine, if using, or water to the pan to deglaze, scraping up the caramelised bits; pour everything into the slow cooker.

4 Add your canned tomatoes and stock to the slow cooker, season. Cover with the lid and cook on low for 8 hours, until the meat is tender and falling apart. In the last 15 minutes, stir in tender veggies and cook until just tender.

5 Remove the meat and set aside. If the sauce is too thin, simmer uncovered until it reaches your preferred consistency. Brighten the flavour with a dash of vinegar, if you like. Shred the meat into chunks using a fork and return it to the sauce. Adjust seasoning to taste.

6 Spoon the ragu over the pappardelle, if using, and toss through. Serve scattered with thyme and oregano leaves, and grated parmesan, if using.

STORE Freeze ragu in an airtight container for up to 3 months.

Saveful tips

Any stewing meat will work well; try beef chuck or cheek, pork shoulder, boneless lamb shoulder, boneless lamb leg or lamb shanks.

Experiment with flavours by working with herbs and spices. For Indian flavours, think cumin, turmeric, chilli and coriander. For Mexican, try chipotle, cumin, coriander and paprika.

prep + cook time 45 minutes + marinating **serves** 4

Piri Piri chicken

Piri-Piri is the smoky, spicy all-rounder that brings sizzle to summer barbecues and warmth to winter nights.

Ingredients

600g chicken thigh cutlets or chicken breast fillets

Marinade

3 deseeded long red chillis, finely chopped (see Saveful tips)

6 cloves garlic, crushed, 4 tsp garlic paste or 2 tsp garlic powder

3 tsp smoked paprika or paprika

¼ bunch thyme or lemon thyme, leaves only, or 1 tbsp dried thyme, optional

⅓ cup neutral oil

⅓ cup lemon or lime juice

finishing touches, to serve: lemon wedges and chipotle mayonnaise, optional

Make it

1 Cut your chicken into 75g portions and lightly score to allow marinade to seep in. Refrigerate while making the marinade.

2 To make the marinade: Blend your chillies, garlic, paprika and herbs, if using, until finely chopped. With the motor running, drizzle in the olive oil to form a paste, then add your juice and process to combine. (If you're using chilli flakes instead of fresh chilli, add extra oil to loosen.) Season with salt.

3 Preheat oven to 200°C fan-forced. Line a baking tray with baking paper.

4 Combine your chicken with the marinade in a large bowl, mixing well to coat. Cover and marinate in the fridge for at least 30 minutes (or longer if preferred). Remove chicken from fridge 30 minutes before you're ready to start cooking.

5 Place chicken on the lined baking tray. Roast for 25–30 minutes until cooked through. (Alternatively, cook on the barbecue on medium heat, covered, for 20–25 minutes, turning every 5–10 minutes for even colour.) Rest chicken for 5 minutes before transferring to a serving plate.

6 Finish chicken with lemon wedges and chipotle mayonnaise, if using.

Saveful tips

Substitute fresh chillies with 1–2 tsp chilli flakes, ground chilli or chilli paste, to taste.

This piri-piri marinade works beautifully with fish fillets, beef, pork or lamb steaks and even on vegetable steaks such as cauliflower or pumpkin.

prep + cook time 25 minutes **serves** 4

Go-to Mexican-inspired chilli

The joy of a great chilli mixture is how versatile it is. Nachos or tacos? You choose.

Ingredients

2 tbsp neutral oil

½ cup finely chopped aromatics (choose 1–2: onion, shallot, spring onions)

2 garlic cloves crushed or 2 tsp garlic paste

2 tbsp flavour booster (tomato paste or finely chopped sundried tomatoes), optional

1 cup finely grated or chopped veggies (carrot, zucchini or button mushrooms), optional

1½ tbsp ground spices (choose 2–3: cumin, coriander, smoked paprika)

1–2 tsp ground chilli or chilli flakes, optional

500g beef or chicken mince (see Saveful tips)

400g can black beans or kidney beans, optional

400g can chopped tomatoes or canned cherry tomatoes

2 tsp lime juice or white wine vinegar

170g pkt corn chips

1–1½ cups grated cheese (cheddar, Mexican blend, mozzarella)

finishing touches, to serve: sliced avocado, fresh tomato salsa, coriander sprigs and lime wedges

Make it

1 Preheat oven to 200°C fan-forced.

2 Heat your oil in a large saucepan on a medium-high heat. Add your aromatics and garlic and a pinch of salt. Cook, stirring occasionally until onion begins to soften, about 3–4 minutes.

3 Add your flavour booster, if using, and cook for 1–2 minutes to bring out the flavours. Then add in your grated or chopped veggies, if using. Stir in your spices to release the aromas. Your kitchen will be starting to smell heavenly by now! Add ground chilli to taste, if using, and cook for another minute.

4 Add your mince to the pan and stir to break it up and brown well, about 5 minutes. Add the canned beans with the liquid to the pan, if using, and stir to combine.

5 Add the canned tomatoes to the pan, bring to a simmer and cook, stirring occasionally, until mixture is thick and well-flavoured about 6–8 minutes. Add lime juice or vinegar, to taste, and simmer for a further 1–2 minutes. Taste and adjust the seasoning.

6 Turn your chilli into nachos: Spread corn chips over a large shallow rectangular baking dish. Spoon chilli over corn chips then scatter with grated cheese. Bake for 5–6 minutes until cheese is melted. Finish with avocado slices, fresh tomato salsa and lime wedges on the side.

STORE Freeze chilli in an airtight container for up to 3 months.

Saveful Tips

For a vegetarian version, swap the beef mince with plant-based mince or 500g drained finely grated tofu.

To turn your chilli into tacos: serve on warmed mini tortillas, topped with mashed avocado, crumbled feta, fresh tomato salsa, shredded red cabbage and lime wedges.

Saveful Tips

Use any protein you have on hand: chicken, pork, beef or plant-based mince, bacon, canned tuna, chorizo, cooked prawns, roast chicken, roast pork, salami. The possibilities are endless.

prep + cook time 20 minutes **serves** 4

Tomato-y pasta

Paired-back or layered-up, a tomato-based pasta is such an easy, flexible and delicious dinner.

Ingredients

- 4 Italian-style or garlic & fennel sauages (see Saveful tips)
- 2 tbsp olive oil
- 1 small brown or red onion, finely chopped
- 2–3 cloves garlic, crushed or 2 tsp garlic paste
- 1–2 tsp flavour booster (choose 1–2: dried chilli flakes, dried oregano, fennel seeds, mixed Italian herbs or 1–2 chopped anchovies)
- ⅓ cup finely chopped veggies (choose 1–2: capsicum, celery, fennel), optional
- 2 large tomatoes, chopped (or 400g can chopped tomatoes or cherry tomatoes or 1½ cups passata)
- ¼ cup red or white wine, optional
- 400g penne pasta or gluten-free penne
- 2 leaves kale or silverbeet, sliced, optional
- 1–2 tbsp coarsely chopped fresh herbs (choose 1–2: parsley, basil, oregano, thyme)
- 1–2 tsp red wine vinegar or lemon juice, to taste, optional
- ½ cup finely grated cheese (parmesan, mozzarella)

Make it

1 Place a large saucepan of well-salted water over a high heat and bring to the boil.

2 Squeeze sausage meat from casings and break into small meatball size pieces. Heat your oil in a large, deep frying pan over medium-high heat and add sausage meat, stirring occasionally to brown well, about 3–4 minutes. Transfer to a plate using a slotted spoon and set aside.

3 Add your onion to the same pan and sauté, until softened, about 4–5 minutes. Stir in the garlic and cook for 30 seconds. Add your chosen flavour booster and chopped veggies, season and sauté until they are softened, about 4–5 minutes.

4 Add your tomatoes and simmer until the tomatoes begin to break down, about 5 minutes. Add your wine here, if using, then bring back to a simmer and season.

5 While your sauce simmers, add the pasta to the boiling water, stir to stop it sticking together or to the bottom of the pan, and cook following the packet directions until al dente. Drain your pasta, reserving ½ cup of the pasta cooking water, and return pasta to the saucepan.

6 Add your kale or silverbeet, if using, to your sauce and simmer until wilted, about 3–4 minutes. Stir in vinegar or lemon juice, if using. Return sausage meat to sauce in frying pan and simmer until heated through, about 2–3 minutes.

7 Add the cooked pasta to the sauce, stir to coat well, thin with a little of the reserved pasta water, if you like. Stir a handful of grated cheese through the sauce.

8 Serve pasta topped with remaining grated cheese.

STORE Freeze sauce in an airtight container for up to 3 months.

prep + cook time 1 hour **serves** 4

Saucy salmon curry tray bake

Looking for a one-tray wonder with plenty of saucy lusciousness?

Ingredients

⅓ cup Thai curry paste, or to taste (choose 1: red curry, green curry, yellow curry)

400g can coconut milk or coconut cream

2 cups Campbell's Real Stock (Chicken or Vegetable), or water

2–3 tsp fish sauce or salt, to taste, optional

2–3 tsp lime or lemon juice, to taste, optional

2–3 tbsp finely chopped aromatics (choose 2: shallot, garlic, ginger), optional

1–2 tsp sweetener, to taste (brown sugar, coconut sugar, palm sugar, or honey), optional

400g hardy veggies, cut into wedges (choose 2–3: pumpkin, red onion, sweet potato, potato, carrot)

1⅓ cups tender veggies (broccoli, capsicum, eggplant, mushrooms), optional

1–2 bunches super tender veg (broccolini, asparagus or bok choy)

4 x 180g skinned and pin boned salmon, ocean trout or firm white fish fillets

finishing touches, to serve: lime or lemon halves and fried shallots

Make it

1 Combine your curry paste, coconut milk and stock in a jug and mix well. Stir in the fish sauce, juice, sweetener and aromatics, if using. Pour into a large shallow rectangular roasting pan.

2 Toss hardy veggies in a little oil and arrange in the sauce. Roast for 20 minutes until veggies are beginning to soften. Toss your tender veg, if using, in a little more oil, season then scatter over the partly-cooked veggies in the pan. Roast for another 15 minutes.

3 Place super tender veg and fish fillets on veggies and cook until all veggies are tender and fish is cooked and tender, about 10–12 minutes.

4 Serve salmon curry finished with lime halves and scattered with fried shallots.

Saveful Tips

Balance your curry with sugar, salt and acid for that perfect Thai curry flavour.

prep + cook time 1 hour 50 minutes **serves** 4

Veggie bolognese

Rich, hearty, and packed with flavour — a flexible classic that keeps on giving.

Ingredients

¼ cup neutral oil

1 cup finely chopped aromatics (choose 1–2: onion, leek, shallots)

¾ cup diced aromatic veggies (choose 1–2: carrot, celery, fennel)

2–3 cloves garlic crushed or 1–2 tsp garlic paste

500g plant-based protein (plant-based mince, canned drained and rinsed lentils or chopped firm tofu)

3 cups finely chopped or grated extra veggies (choose 2–4: mushrooms, cauliflower, pumpkin, sweet potato, zucchini)

2 x 400g cans chopped tomatoes or cherry tomatoes

1½ cups Campbell's Real Stock Vegetable

½ cup white or red wine, optional

1–2 tsp dried oregano, thyme or bay leaf or 1–2 tbsp chopped fresh oregano or thyme

1–2 tsp balsamic or red wine vinegar, optional

1–2 tsp white or brown sugar, optional

400g dried long pasta (fettuccine, tagliatelle or spaghetti)

finishing touches, to serve: grated parmesan

Make it

1 Heat a generous splash of oil in a large, heavy-based saucepan over medium-high heat. Add your aromatics, aromatic veggies and garlic; sauté, stirring occasionally, until tender, about 5 minutes. Season generously with salt and pepper.

2 Add your plant-based protein, breaking it up with a wooden spoon and cook, stirring occasionally, for 5–6 minutes until it is browned.

3 Stir in your extra vegetables and cook until softened, about 6–8 minutes. Add your canned tomatoes, stock and wine, if using, and stir to combine. Simmer for 5 minutes, then stir in your herbs.

4 Reduce the heat to medium and simmer gently, stirring occasionally, for about 1 hour until the sauce is thick and rich.

5 Add vinegar and sugar, if using ,and adjust balance as needed. Season and simmer for another 5–10 minutes.

6 Meanwhile, cook your pasta in a large saucepan of generously salted boiling water following packet instructions until al dente. Drain, reserving 1 cup of pasta cooking water. Stir the drained pasta through the bolognese sauce, adding a little of the pasta water if needed.

7 Serve pasta and sauce, topped with grated parmesan.

STORE Freeze bolognese in portions in airtight containers for up to 3 months.

Saveful tips

This bolognese has so many lives. Turn it into a lasagne, cannelloni, cottage pie or simply spoon over baked jacket potatoes and more!

Weekends

prep time 20 minutes **serves** 8–10

Any veg hummus

Hummus is more than a dip — it's your fridge-cleaning, crowd-pleasing hero.

Ingredients

400g can chickpeas

½ cup tahini or almond butter, optional

2–3 cloves garlic or 1 tsp garlic paste

1–1½ cups veggies (choose 1–2: grated carrot, roasted pumpkin or sweet potato, canned or roasted beetroot, roasted cauliflower, blanched peas, blanched broccoli) (see Saveful tips)

⅓ cup lemon juice, or to taste

2–3 tbsp olive oil, plus extra for drizzling or water

finishing touches, to serve: pita crisps, crostini, blanched asparagus, carrot batons, halved baby cucumbers and radishes

Make it

1 Drain your chickpeas and reserve the liquid. Add the chickpeas to a food processor or blender, then add your tahini, if using, garlic and veggies. Add 2–3 tablespoons of lemon juice and 2 tablespoons reserved chickpea liquid or water.

2 Pour in the oil, if using (it will give a silky smooth consistency), or use remaining chickpea liquid, or water, if you prefer. Season generously with salt and pepper. Process mixture, scraping down sides once or twice, until it is super smooth.

3 Taste, add a little more lemon juice and seasoning if needed, then process to combine.

4 Drizzle hummus with a little extra oil and serve with pita crisps, crostini, blanched asparagus, carrot batons, halved baby cucumbers and radishes.

STORE Keep hummus refrigerated in an airtight container for up to 5 days. Or freeze in ½ cup portions in snap lock bags for up to 3 months.

Saveful Tips

Use leftover roast veggies here, or toss chopped hardy veggies in oil and roast at 200°C fan-forced for 25–30 minutes until caramelised and tender. Steam or blanch green veggies.

Leftover makeover: Make a hummus veggie bowl. Spoon a big dollop of your hummus in a shallow bowl, top with diced crunchy veg (use up any of those crudites you may have served with it, think carrot, cucumber, tomato, radish and onion) and drizzle with a squeeze of lemon and olive oil). Top with a boiled egg, or leftover roast chicken or lamb and lunch or dinner is done!

prep + cook time 45 minutes **serves** 6

Classic seafood paella

Big on flavour, easy on rules — this paella is an absolute showstopper you can totally make your own.

Ingredients

2 tbsp olive oil

¾ cup chopped aromatics (choose 1–2: onion, shallots, spring onions)

1 clove of garlic or ¼ tsp garlic paste

1½ cups arborio, bomba or medium grain rice (see Saveful tips)

1–2 tsp paprika or smoked paprika

½ cup chopped raw veggies (carrots, trimmed green beans)

¾ cup canned diced or cherry tomatoes

3 cups Campbell's Real Stock (Chicken, Vegetable or Fish), plus extra if needed (see Saveful tips)

½ cup chopped cooked veggies (roasted capsicum, roasted sweet potato)

500g mixed seafood (peeled green prawns, calamari rings, cleaned mussels, chopped skinned and deboned firm white fish fillet or marinara mix) (see Saveful tips)

¼ cup frozen peas

finishing touches, to serve: 3 cooked king prawns, chopped fresh parsley or oregano and lemon wedges

Make it

1 Heat oil in a 30cm flat-bottomed frying pan or paella pan over high heat. Add your aromatics and garlic and cook until just softened, about 3 minutes.

2 Stir in your rice to coat in oil. Add paprika and raw veggies and stir through the rice. Add your tomatoes and stock and stir to combine. Bring to the boil, then reduce heat to a gentle simmer. Simmer for about 10 minutes without stirring. It's important not to stir the rice, the stock will reduce and caramelise along with the rice, making the all-important crust on the base of the pan (the socarrat).

3 Add your cooked veggies to the rice. Top with seafood then add your peas. Cover with a lid and cook for another 10 minutes.

4 Remove pan from the heat and finish with cooked king prawns, fresh herbs, and lemon wedges.

Saveful Tips

If using arborio rice, you might need to add 1 extra cup of Campbell's Real Stock and increase cooking time by about 15 minutes.

Not keen on seafood? No worries. Use 600g of your favourite protein (choose 1–3): bacon, chopped chicken thigh fillet, sliced chorizo, chopped tofu. Saute in step 1, remove from pan then, add with cooked veg in step 3 and continue as per recipe.

prep + cook time 1 hour 40 minutes + resting **serves** 4

Perfect roast chook

Who doesn't love a Sunday roast? This juicy, flavour-packed chook is easy to make, and the best bit — the leftovers stretch into another meal (or two!).

Ingredients

2kg whole chook

1 large onion, thickly sliced

6–8 garlic cloves

1–2 tbsp neutral oil

1–2 tsp spice (choose 1–2; dukkah, ground coriander, ground cumin, paprika, ground sumac), optional

1½–2 cups Campbell's Real Stock (Chicken or Vegetable)

½ cup white wine, optional

4–6 large potatoes or sweet potatoes, cut into large wedges

8 Dutch carrots, scrubbed and trimmed or 3 carrots, cut into wedges

Stuffing

6–8 sprigs fresh herbs (choose 1–3: oregano, rosemary, sage, thyme, tarragon)

a few pieces aromatics (choose 1–2: onion, leek, spring onion, or shallots, quartered)

½ lemon, cut into wedges

Gravy

½–1 cup Campbell's Real Stock (Chicken or Vegetable), approximately

½ cup white wine, optional

2 tbsp butter or olive oil

2 tbsp plain or gluten-free plain flour

1 Take your chook out of the fridge half an hour before cooking. Pat dry inside and out with paper towel; do not rinse the chook.

2 Preheat the oven to 220°C fan-forced. Line a baking tray with baking paper and lightly oil a roasting pan big enough to fit your chook with a little bit of space around it.

3 Fill the cavity of your chicken with stuffing ingredients, including the lemon wedges, to give it extra flavour. Tie the legs together with kitchen string (unwaxed) if you like, to help the chicken cook evenly.

4 Place onion and garlic in the roasting pan and drizzle with oil. Drizzle more oil over your chicken and season generously with salt and pepper. Sprinkle with spice, if using, and rub into chicken. Place your chicken on top of onion. Pour your stock and wine, if using, around the chicken; this will help keep it moist.

5 Place potatoes and carrots on the lined baking tray, season and drizzle with oil; toss to combine. Set aside.

6 Roast your chook for 20 minutes. Reduce the oven to 180°C fan-forced and roast for another 1 hour 20 minutes until golden brown and cooked through. Pierce the thigh with a skewer, press gently to release the juices, if juices have a pink tinge, you'll need to cook the chicken a bit longer. If the juices are clear, your chook is done. Transfer your chicken to a tray and let it rest for 20 minutes.

7 Place your veg in the oven at the same time you reduce the temp; toss halfway through cooking and check after 1 hour.

8 While your chook is resting, make the gravy: Pour the roasting pan juices into a measuring jug and top up to 375ml with stock and wine, if using. Heat butter in a small saucepan, add flour and stir until smooth. Cook for 1–2 minutes, then gradually add your stock mixture, whisking until smooth and combined. Whisk over medium-high heat for another couple of minutes until it has thickened. Mash the roast garlic from your pan and whisk into the gravy and season to taste.

9 Serve chicken with roast veggies and gravy, and steamed peas on the side, if you like.

Saveful Tips

The no-fail formula for cooking a chicken to perfection is to cook it for the first 20 minutes at 220°C fan-forced. Reduce the oven to 180°C and continue to cook for 20 minutes for every 500g.

If your roasting pan dries out, add more liquid (water, stock or wine) to top it up. Keep an eye on your onion and garlic too and remove from the pan if they cook before the chicken.

Saveful Tips

Focaccia is traditionally made with yeast; if you don't have it, you can use 4 tsp baking powder or use self-raising flour instead of plain. The flavour and texture will be more like a damper or savoury scone dough but it will still be tasty. No proving is necessary. Place in tin, top and bake.

Swap in your favourite toppings, try asparagus, bacon, ham, potato, pumpkin, salami, zucchini.

prep + cook time 2 hours + proving **serves** 8

Savoury easy peasy focaccia

Crispy on the outside, fluffy on the inside — focaccia is the no-fuss bread that turns simple ingredients into bakery-worthy magic.

Ingredients

4 cups plain flour (or a mix of white and wholemeal)

1–2 tsp salt

7g sachet instant dried yeast (see Saveful tips)

2½ cups lukewarm water

1–2 tbsp olive oil, plus 2–3 tbsp extra

¼ cup grated, crumbled or torn cheese (cheddar, mozzarella, feta or bocconcini)

¼ cup toppings (cherry tomatoes or olives, sliced mixed mushrooms and rosemary sprigs)

Make it

1 Add flour and salt in a large mixing bowl. Add the yeast and mix to combine. Make a well in the centre of your dry mixture. Pour your lukewarm water into the well then add your oil.

2 Mix the dry and wet ingredients together to just combine; your dough will be shaggy, rough and quite wet. No need to overmix.

3 Lightly oil a clean large bowl; tip your dough into the bowl and drizzle with a little more oil, lightly covering the surface to prevent a crust forming. Cover with plastic wrap or a clean tea towel. Stand at room temperature for 1–2 hours or overnight in the fridge to proof until it is doubled in size.

4 Oil a 20–25cm x 30–35cm baking pan. Tip dough into the pan and gently stretch toward the edges. Stand at room temperature to proof for 1 hour or until risen and puffy.

5 Preheat oven to 200°C fan-forced.

6 Use oiled fingers to press dimples all over the dough. Drizzle the top of the focaccia with a generous glug of olive oil! Scatter your cheese and toppings evenly over your dough, season to taste and drizzle with a little more oil.

7 Bake your focaccia for 20–25 minutes until puffy and golden brown. Cool in the pan for 10 minutes. Transfer to a wire rack and eat warm or at room temperature.

STORE Freeze portions of focaccia individually wrapped in plastic wrap for up to 1 month.

prep + cook time 30 minutes **serves** 4

Creamy tangy potato salad

Creamy, zesty, and downright irresistible, this potato salad steals the show! It's perfect for a barbecue or summer's day picnic.

Ingredients

4 large or 12–16 baby potatoes
¼ cup chopped crispy bacon
¼ cup sliced pickles
1⅓ cups blanched extra veggies (choose 1–2: asparagus, frozen edamame, frozen peas, green beans, snow peas, sugar snap peas), optional
3 boiled eggs, peeled, quartered

Creamy tangy dressing
½ cup mayonnaise or aïoli
½ cup yoghurt (Greek-style, natural or coconut), sour cream or crème fraîche
2–4 tsp lemon or lime juice or your favourite vinegar
1–2 tbsp chopped fresh herbs (choose 1–3: basil, chives, dill, mint or parsley), plus extra to finish
⅓ cup finely chopped aromatics (spring onions, or red or white onion)

Make it

1 Cut large potatoes into 3–4cm chunks and halve any larger baby potatoes. Place potatoes in a large saucepan, cover with cold water, generously salt the water, then bring to the boil. Cook about 8–10 minutes until a skewer inserts easily into the potatoes. Drain. Cool slightly.
2 To make the creamy tangy dressing: Place mayonnaise and yoghurt in a bowl, stir to combine. Season with salt and pepper, then add your juice or vinegar to taste. Stir in herbs and aromatics.
3 Add the dressing to the cooked potatoes and toss gently to combine. Add your bacon, pickles and blanched veggies, if using, toss gently to combine.
4 Serve potato salad topped with egg quarters and scattered with extra herbs.

Saveful Tips

Don't have bacon, eggs or pickles? Don't worry, add capers, chorizo, ham, olives, or pickled onion instead.

Italian butter

prep time 10 minutes

Combine 250g softened butter with 1–2 cloves roasted garlic or 1 tsp garlic powder or paste, ½ tsp each of dried thyme, dried rosemary and mixed Italian herbs. Shape into a log and wrap firmly in plastic wrap or roll into balls and place in an airtight container; refrigerate for up to 1 week or freeze for up to 2 months.

Smoked chilli & pickle butter

prep time 10 minutes

Combine 250g softened butter with 2 tbsp chopped pickles (cucumber pickles, gherkins, mustard pickles or kimchi), 1 tsp chilli flakes or chopped fresh red chilli and 2 tsp paprika. Shape into a log and wrap firmly in plastic wrap or roll into balls and place in an airtight container; refrigerate for up to 1 week or freeze for up to 2 months.

Indian-spiced chutney butter

prep time 10 minutes

Combine 250g softened butter with 2 tbsp chutney (mango, tomato, fruit), 1 tsp ground spice (curry powder, garam marsala, cumin or coriander), ½ tsp turmeric and 1 crushed clove garlic or ½ tsp garlic paste. Shape into a log and wrap firmly in plastic wrap or roll into balls and place in an airtight container; refrigerate for up to 1 week or freeze for up to 2 months.

prep + cook time 2 hours **serves** 4

Excellent roast vegetables

Roast potatoes might be the classic, but it's time to let the whole veggie drawer join the crispy, golden party.

Ingredients

1kg hardy vegetables (choose 1–5: baby carrots, beetroot, fennel, parsnip, potato, sweet potato, pumpkin, or swede)

2–3 tbsp neutral oil

1 onion, cut into wedges or 4 shallots, halved

1 whole bulb garlic, halved horizontally

2 sprigs of fresh thyme or rosemary

finishing touches, to serve: roasted pumpkin seeds, chopped almonds and pesto, optional

Make it

1 Preheat your oven to 180°C fan-forced. Line two large baking trays with baking paper.

2 Peel the beetroot, parsnip, pumpkin and swede if using. Then cut these and the other veggies you are using into chunks roughly the same size and chunkier than you think, as they'll shrink by about 30%.

3 Combine all the hardy vegetables except beetroot in a large bowl. Drizzle your veggies with a generous amount of oil, season with salt and pepper; toss to coat evenly. Repeat with beetroot, if using. Spread your veg in a single layer onto the lined trays, making sure you don't overcrowd the trays.

4 Roast for 20 minutes. Add your onion, garlic and fresh herbs, then toss gently to combine. Roast for another 30–90 minutes until caramelised and tender; roasting time depends on which veggies you have and how big you have cut them. Be sure to keep checking on them until they are roasted to perfection.

5 Finish roast vegetables with roasted pumpkin seeds, chopped almonds and pesto, if using.

Saveful Tips

Opt for shallow baking trays if you have them as the veggies will caramelise better.

Leftover roast veg can be used in salads, curries, frittatas, or stirred into a hearty chunky soup to make getting your five daily serves even easier.

prep + cook time 35 minutes **serves** 4

Eggy bread bake

Got bread and bits to use up? Our Eggy bread bake turns leftovers into golden, cheesy, bubbling goodness that's perfect for a weekend brunch or picnic.

Ingredients

6–8 thick slices leftover bread (sandwich loaf, sourdough, or Turkish bread) (see Saveful tips)

2 tbsp neutral oil or butter

½ cup thinly sliced aromatics (choose 1–2: onion, shallots, spring onion, leek)

1–2 tbsp fresh chopped herbs (choose 1–2: oregano, rosemary or thyme, chives), optional

1–1½ cups veggies (cherry tomatoes, sliced mushrooms, chopped broccolini, sundried tomatoes)

4–6 slices streaky bacon or prosciutto, optional

5 eggs

1¼ cups dairy or plant-based liquid (milk, cream, sour cream, natural yoghurt, crème fraîche) (see Saveful tips)

1–2 tbsp Dijon or seeded mustard, or fruit chutney, optional

1 cup grated or crumbled cheese (cheddar, parmesan, haloumi, feta, or goats cheese)

finishing touches, to serve: mashed avocado, lemon wedges and chopped chives, optional

Make it

1 Preheat your oven to 180°C fan-forced. Lightly grease a 13.5cm x 26.5cm standard loaf tin.

2 Roughly tear your bread and place it into the tin.

3 Heat the oil or butter in a large frying pan over medium heat. Add your aromatics and cook until they're softened and golden, about 4–5 minutes. Stir in your herbs, if using, and your veggies, cook until lightly softened, about 3–4 minutes.

4 Spoon veggie mixture evenly over the bread, tucking some between the slices. Layer with bacon or prosciutto.

5 In a large bowl, whisk eggs, your liquid and mustard or chutney, if using, until well combined. Stir in your cheese. Season with salt and pepper.

6 Pour the egg and cheese mixture evenly over the bread, allowing it to soak in. Bake for about 30 minutes, until puffed, golden, and just set to the touch.

7 Serve sliced eggy bread with mashed avocado, lemon wedges and chopped chives, if using.

Saveful Tips

Any bread will work here, even bread rolls, bagels or baguettes. Older bread is best as it soaks up the egg mixture better than fresh bread.

If using sour cream, yoghurt, or crème fraîche as your liquid, loosen with a splash of water to the consistency of thickened cream before adding.

prep + cook time 1 hour 20 minutes **serves** 12

Loaded fudgy brownies

Brownies are fudgy, gooey, choc-loaded bliss. Bonus points — this batch sneaks in some veg so you can have your cake and secretly eat your veggies too!

Ingredients

250g chocolate, chopped (dark, milk, dairy free or choc chips)

250g fat (butter, coconut oil, vegetable oil or mashed avocado) (see Saveful tips)

1 cup sugar (brown, caster, white or coconut)

4 eggs

1 cup sneaky grated veggies (carrot, beetroot, sweet potato, zucchini), optional

1¼ cups plain flour (wholemeal, gluten-free, spelt, almond meal or hazelnut meal)

¼ tsp baking powder

1⅓ cups mix-ins (choose 1–3: berries, cacao nibs, choc chips, dried cranberries, dried sour cherries, hazelnuts, almonds, macadamias or pretzels)

Make it

1 Preheat oven to 180°C fan-forced. Grease and line a 20cm square cake tin with baking paper (see Saveful tips).

2 Bring a saucepan of water to a simmer. Place your chocolate and fat in a heatproof bowl over the saucepan and stir until both are melted and smooth. Remove bowl from heat. Stir in the sugar until it is well combined.

3 Add your eggs, one at a time, stirring gently after each addition; be careful not to overmix. Fold in your sneaky grated veg, if using.

4 Sift your flour, baking powder, and a pinch of salt over the mixture and stir until everything is just combined. Fold through 1 cup of your mix-ins until combined. Spoon your batter into the prepared tin, smooth the top, then scatter with your remaining mix-ins.

5 Bake for about 45–50 minutes, until the edges are set but the centre is still slightly fudgy. Cool completely in the tin before cutting into pieces.

STORE Freeze cut brownie in an airtight container for up to 2 months.

Saveful Tips

If using avocado as the fat, stir it in after the chocolate has melted.

If you are using a slice tin, your brownies will be thinner and take less time to cook. You can even bake them in an ovenproof skillet and serve warm at the table for dessert.

prep + cook time 50 minutes + standing **serves** 4–6

Fruity crumble

Few desserts are easier or more comforting than a crumble with its sweet fruit filling and crunchy topping — perfectly adaptable to any season. It's a great way to use up apples, pears, or rhubarb.

Ingredients

6–7 cups fruit (chopped apples, chopped pears, chopped rhubarb, fresh or frozen berries)

½–¾ cup sugar (brown, white, caster or rapadura), to taste

1–2 tbsp citrus juice (orange, lemon or lime), to taste

1–2 tbsp cornflour

1–2 tsp vanilla (bean paste, extract or essence), optional

Crumble topping

1 cup plain flour (white, wholemeal or gluten-free)

½ cup sugar (brown, coconut, rapadura or demerara)

125g chilled, diced butter or plant-based butter

2–3 tsp ground spices (choose 1–2: cinnamon, ginger, nutmeg, mixed spice), optional

¼–⅓ cup crunch (choose 1–4: chopped almonds, hazelnuts or walnuts; desiccated or shredded coconut; granola or oats), optional

finishing touches, to serve: ice-cream, yoghurt, cream or sour cream, optional

Make it

1 Preheat your oven to 180°C fan-forced. Lightly grease a deep 23cm round or 20cm x 30cm baking dish.

2 To make crumble topping: Pop your flour, sugar, butter and a pinch of salt in a bowl. Add your spices, if using. Rub mixture together with your fingertips until clusters form (or give it a few pulses in the food processor for a quicker mix). Stir in your crunch ingredients, if using. Set aside.

3 For the fruit filling, put your fruit, sugar, citrus juice and cornflour in a large bowl and mix well to combine. Stir in your vanilla, if using. Tip into your baking dish. Scatter the crumble topping evenly over the fruit.

4 Pop the dish on a baking-paper-lined baking tray to catch any drips and bake for 30–40 minutes until golden and bubbling. If the top browns too quickly, cover with foil and keep baking until the fruit softens. Check the fruit is tender by sliding in a knife or skewer.

5 Let the fruity crumble stand for 15 minutes before serving (trust us, it thickens up beautifully and saves burnt tongues). Serve with ice-cream, yoghurt, cream, or even a dollop of sour cream for tang.

Saveful Tips

Any fruit works well here, try apples, pears, rhubarb, fresh or frozen berries, stone fruit, even canned fruit. Just mix and match what you've got.

If you don't have enough butter, you can swap out some of the butter for tahini, peanut butter or other nut butter.

prep + cook time 3 hours + overnight refrigeration **serves** 6–8

Roast pork

This roast is a guaranteed crowd-pleaser, with its perfectly crisp and crunchy crackling, and meltingly tender meat.

Ingredients

2–2.5kg boneless pork loin, pork belly or pork shoulder

1–2 tsp sea salt flakes

Garlic-herb paste

6–8 cloves fresh garlic, crushed or 3–4 tsp garlic paste

2–3 tbsp finely chopped fresh herbs (choose 1–3: oregano, thyme, sage)

2–3 tbsp oil

1–2 tsp flavour booster (choose 1–2: caraway seeds, dried chilli flakes, fennel seeds, finely grated lemon or orange rind)

finishing touches, to serve: roast veggies, cos lettuce wedges, and fruity relish, optional

Make it

1 Pat your pork dry with paper towel. Place it skin-side up on a clean work surface; using a very sharp small knife or scalpel, score the skin at 1.5-2cm apart or ask your butcher to do this for you. Sprinkle a teaspoon of salt over the pork skin. Place skin-side up on a baking tray and refrigerate overnight to allow skin to dry out for perfect crackling.

2 To make garlic-herb paste: Combine all the ingredients in a small bowl; season to taste generously with sea salt and freshly ground pepper, then mix well.

3 Preheat the oven to 220°C fan-forced.

4 Remove your pork from fridge. Pat skin dry with paper towel. Turn your pork over and rub garlic-herb paste over the flesh. Roll it into a tight cylinder from one of the short sides, there shouldn't be any skin on the inside of the roll, so if there is, unroll the cylinder and trim off the skin that was inside (don't throw it away). Re-roll the pork, then tie at regular intervals with kitchen string (unwaxed) to secure.

5 Rub the pork skin generously with sea salt flakes, ensuring the salt is rubbed into the scoring cuts. Place the pork on a wire rack in a roasting pan and roast for 30 minutes. If you have the skin offcut, add to the oven now and remove as soon as it's crisp and crunchy. Reduce the oven temperature to 180°C fan-forced and roast for another 25 minutes per kilo. Rest your pork for 30 minutes.

6 Pour any pan juices from the pan into a jug. Skim off the fat with a spoon (reserve fat in a container in the fridge to use another time for the crunchiest roast potatoes ever!).

7 Serve roast pork with the pan juices, finishing with roast veggies, cos lettuce wedges and fruity relish, if using.

prep + cook time 55 minutes **serves** 8

Bread & butter pudding

Nothing says comfort like a bread and butter pudding. Soft, custardy layers under a crunchy top. Even better, it's the perfect way to give leftover bread a second life.

Ingredients

12 slices leftover bread (challah, brioche loaf, fruit bread, sandwich bread, croissants, burger buns or potato buns, or hot dog rolls)

60–80g softened butter

¼ cup marmalade, optional

1½ cups dairy or plant-based milk

4 eggs

1–2 tbsp sweetener (brown, caster or white sugar, honey or maple syrup)

2 tsp flavour boosters (choose 1–3: cinnamon, nutmeg, finely grated lemon rind, vanilla)

½ cup blueberries (fresh, frozen or dried) (see Saveful tips)

finishing touches, to serve: icing sugar, whipped cream, extra fresh blueberries and shredded lemon rind, optional

Make it

1 Preheat your oven to 180°C fan-forced. Grease a 2.5 litre (10-cup) capacity baking dish with a little butter.

2 Spread sliced bread with butter and marmalade, if using.

3 Gently warm your milk in a saucepan over low heat, or in the microwave. Don't let it boil, it just needs to warm through. Whisk your eggs, sweetener and flavour boosters together to combine; stir in your warmed milk.

4 Layer your bread slices into your baking dish, scattering the blueberries between layers. Pour over your egg mixture and stand for 5 minutes to soak.

5 Bake until golden brown on the top and just set with a bit of a wobble; for larger baking dishes this will take 25–30 minutes. If your baking dish is deeper it may take a little longer, check after 15 minutes. Stand your pudding for 10 minutes before serving.

6 Serve pudding finished with a dusting of icing sugar, a dollop of whipped cream, extra fresh blueberries, and some shredded lemon rind, if using.

Saveful Tips

Swap blueberries with any fresh, frozen or dried berry. Use stone fruits when in season, such as peaches, apricots, plums or cherries. Add chocolate for extra indulgence or chopped nuts for texture.

If you're using dried fruit, poke any floating pieces under the surface, as they can burn easily.

prep + cook time 1 hour **serves** 8–10 (makes 1 pizza)

Sheet pan pizza

Sheet pan pizza is a fuss-free way to cater for a crowd. There's no rolling individual pizzas, and serving a whole slab at once is an impressive table centre-piece.

Ingredients

3 cups self-raising flour or 3 cups plain flour plus 1½ tbsp baking powder

1½ cups Greek-style or natural yoghurt

1–2 tbsp olive oil

Red sauce

⅓ cup tomato passata or canned diced tomatoes

1–2 cloves garlic, crushed or 1 tsp garlic paste

1–2 tbsp olive oil, to taste

1–2 tbsp finely chopped fresh herbs or 1–2 tsp dried (basil, parsley oregano, or thyme), optional

Tomato & prosciutto topping

¼–⅓ cup red sauce

1 cup grated, crumbled or torn cheese (mozzarella, feta, ricotta, cheddar, tasty)

1½–2 cups tomato medley or cherry tomatoes, halved

4–6 slices prosciutto

a handful of fresh basil leaves

Zucchini & ricotta topping

1–1½ cups thinly sliced zucchini

1 cup grated cheese (cheddar, tasty or mozzarella)

¾–1 cup fresh ricotta

a handful of fresh mint leaves

Make it

1 Preheat the oven to 200°C fan-forced. Grease a large baking tray (about 25cm x 40cm) with oil.

2 Combine the flour in a large bowl with 2 tsp salt; make a well in the centre. Add your yoghurt and oil to the well, then mix to form a soft dough. Turn onto a lightly floured surface and knead lightly until just smooth. Rest the dough for about 20 minutes.

3 Roll out your dough on a floured surface until large enough to fit your baking tray. Transfer the dough to the baking tray, pressing and stretching into the corners if necessary.

4 To make red sauce: Combine ingredients in a bowl. Season.

5 If using the tomato & prosciutto topping: Spread the pizza base with enough red sauce to cover. Scatter with cheese and tomatoes. Pop your pizza in the oven and bake until golden brown and bubbling, about 20–30 minutes. Remove from oven and top with prosciutto and basil leaves. Serve straightaway.

6 If using the zucchini & ricotta topping: Top the pizza base with sliced zucchini and scatter with your grated cheese. Pop pizza in the oven and bake until golden brown and bubbling, about 20–30 minutes. Remove from oven and dollop with fresh ricotta, top with mint leaves and sprinkle with cracked black pepper. Serve straightaway.

STORE Freeze individual pieces of leftover pizza wrapped in plastic wrap for up to 2 months.

Saveful Tips

A little of the toppings go a long way, you don't need to be heavy-handed. It's a great way to use up little bits and pieces of veg and cheese you might have lingering in your fridge.

If you want to make both topping suggestions, you'll need to make two batches of the pizza base.

Conversion chart

MEASURES

One Australian metric measuring cup holds approximately 250ml; one Australian metric tablespoon holds 20ml; one Australian metric teaspoon holds 5ml. The difference between one country's measuring cups and another's is within a two- or three-teaspoon variance and will not affect your cooking results. North America, New Zealand and the United Kingdom use a 15ml tablespoon. All cup and spoon measurements are level.

When measuring liquids, use a clear glass or plastic jug with the metric markings. We use extra-large eggs with an average weight of 60g each.

DRY MEASURES

metric	imperial
15g	½oz
30g	1oz
60g	2oz
90g	3oz
125g	4oz (¼lb)
155g	5oz
185g	6oz
220g	7oz
250g	8oz (½lb)
280g	9oz
315g	10oz
345g	11oz
375g	12oz (¾lb)
410g	13oz
440g	14oz
470g	15oz
500g	16oz (1lb)
750g	24oz (1½lb)
1kg	32oz (2lb)

LIQUID MEASURES

metric	imperial
30ml	1 fluid oz
60ml	2 fluid oz
100ml	3 fluid oz
125ml	4 fluid oz
150ml	5 fluid oz
190ml	6 fluid oz
250ml	8 fluid oz
300ml	10 fluid oz
500ml	16 fluid oz
600ml	20 fluid oz
1000ml (1 litre)	1¾ pints

LENGTH MEASURES

metric	imperial
3mm	⅛in
6mm	¼in
1cm	½in
2cm	¾in
2.5cm	1in
5cm	2in
6cm	2½in
8cm	3in
10cm	4in
13cm	5in
15cm	6in
18cm	7in
20cm	8in
22cm	9in
25cm	10in
28cm	11in
30cm	12in (1ft)

OVEN TEMPERATURES

The temperatures in this book and below are for fan-forced ovens; for conventional ovens, increase the temperature by 10-20 degrees.

	°C (Celsius)	°F (Fahrenheit)
Very slow	80	175
Slow	100	210
Moderately slow	130	260
Moderate	140	280
Moderately hot	160	325
Hot	180	350
Very hot	200	400

Measurements for cake pans are approximate only. Using same-shaped cake pans of a similar size should not affect the outcome of your baking. We measure the inside top of the cake pan to determine size.

Index

Published in 2026 by Are Media Books, Australia.

are

Chief Executive Officer
Jane Huxley

General Manager, Homes & Lifestyle
Jocelin Abbey

Books Director
David Scotto

Creative Director
Hannah Blackmore

Project Editor
Stephanie Kistner

Food Editor
Bronwen Clark

CEO & Co Founder
Kim McDonnell

COO & Co Founder
Mike Chuter

Ambassador & Partner
Matt Moran

Thank you
Saveful Consulting Chefs
Dominique Rizzo, Emma Knowles, Matt Moran

Stylists
Emma Knowles, Peter May

Photography
Alan Benson, Recap Media

Printed in China by C&C Offset Printing Co. Ltd, China.

A catalogue record for this book is available from the National Library of Australia. ISBN 978-1-76122-222-1

Published by Are Media Books, a division of Are Media Pty Limited, 54 Park St, Sydney; GPO Box 4088, Sydney, NSW 2001, Australia
Ph +61 2 9282 8000 www.aremediabooks.com.au

Saveful is proudly supported by

ARDMONA

Campbell's